THE
LOST
GIRLS

WHY A FEMINIST REVOLUTION IN EDUCATION BENEFITS EVERYONE

CHARLOTTE M WOOLLEY

First published 2020

by John Catt Educational Ltd,
15 Riduna Park, Station Road,
Melton, Woodbridge IP12 1QT

Tel: +44 (0) 1394 389850
Fax: +44 (0) 1394 386893
Email: enquiries@johncatt.com
Website: www.johncatt.com

ISBN: 978 1 912906 82 6

Set and designed by John Catt Educational Limited

Reviews

Society is acutely aware of the gaps that women face in terms of visibility, career progression and salaries – there are a lot of initiatives in education and beyond to empower and develop women in leadership. But are we focusing our attention enough on closing these gaps in our schools? *The Lost Girls* shines a spotlight on how our schools can enable the next generation of female leaders and sow these seeds of change. A must-read for everyone who is committed to gender equality and who believes that we need systemic, structural and societal change now.

Hannah Wilson, co-founder of #WomenEd
and founder of LeanInGirlsUK

The Lost Girls is a book we have all needed for a long time. Charlotte makes a profound argument for a feminist education system, saying that this will empower women *and* men to fulfil equal roles both at work and at home. Meticulously researched and overwhelmingly positive and practical, this book should be a cornerstone for how we design our schools as places for both students and staff to thrive.

Jennifer Webb, assistant principal at
Co-op Academy Leeds and author of How to
Teach English Literature: overcoming cultural poverty

Contents

Introduction   7
A word on language   17

Part I: The origins of expectation
1. Biological difference   21
2. Socialisation and performance of gender roles   31

Part II: Exploring the curriculum
3. Extended writing   43
4. Oracy   59
5. English   75
6. STEM   93
7. Languages   111
8. Physical education   119
9. The arts   131

Part III: The whole girl
10. Sexist language and sexual harassment   143
11. Healthy emotions   153
12. Relationships and sex education   169
13. Periods   191
14. Overcoming perfectionism   201
15. Financial literacy   215

Part IV: Modelling the feminist society

16. Feminist leadership   227
17. Family-friendly working   239

Conclusion: what happens next?   253
Acknowledgements   255

Introduction

When a woman says, 'I have nothing to wear!', what she really means is, 'There's nothing here for who I'm supposed to be today' – Caitlin Moran, *How To Be a Woman*

The woman is the most perfect doll that I have dressed with delight and admiration – Karl Lagerfeld

A quick scan of education in the UK might suggest we don't need to worry about girls. The traditional narrative is that girls achieve, boys fail to live up to their potential. This is, according to popular myth, at least partly down to personality. Girls, so it goes, are hard-working; boys chance it all on the last exam. Girls are pliable and cooperative – ideal when asking them to meet a mark scheme. Boys need strategies to keep them in check and make them learn, stop them wasting all that potential. Even when girls show academic improvement compared with boys, there's no frenzy of stories about how brilliant the girls' achievements are. Rather, the stories ask: where did it go wrong for the boys? Because girls *do* perform better academically. They get better GCSE grades. They do more A levels, and get more first-class and postgraduate degrees.

Where are all the women?

But where are these high-flying, academically accomplished young women in the world beyond school? They're not in some of the most powerful or economically successful occupations. They're not becoming CEOs, politicians, or tech and finance leaders. Just six of the FTSE 100 CEOs are female.[1] Meanwhile, 34% of MPs are women and, while that might be more than ever, 45% of them are childless, compared with 28% of their male counterparts.[2] Global companies like Google, Facebook and Amazon all face claims of discrimination and institutional bias, whether it's in their hiring practices or their facial recognition software or even their AI voices, which were condemned by a UN report for sending "a signal that women are obliging, docile and eager-to-please helpers, available at the touch of a button".[3]

And that, right there, is the core of the problem when it comes to girls and their education. For all of the progress made between the suffragettes in the early 20th century and the mid 1970s (and we shouldn't be complacent about that huge achievement) we seem to have slowed to a crawl when it comes to changing the narrative about gender. Too many girls are still being pushed into positions that restrict them, limit their opportunities and, quite honestly, trap them into a spiral of anxiousness, because of the conflicting messages that society is giving them.

It's not just at work that women are missing out. According to the Office for National Statistics, women in 2016 were doing 60% more unpaid work than men[4]. In the 2018 British Social Attitudes Survey, 51% of respondents still favoured mothers either staying home full- or part-time, with less than 0.5% (no, that's not a typo) thinking the same about fathers. Admittedly this was down from 69% in 2012, but it's not exactly

---

1. Frances Ball, "More Steves than women are FTSE 100 CEOs", *Economia*, Institute of Chartered Accountants in England and Wales, 22 August 2019
2. Rosie Campbell, "This ludicrous obsession, parents in parliament: the motherhood trap", *The Huffington Post*, 16 January 2014
3. *I'd Blush If I Could: closing gender divides in digital skills through education*, UNESCO, 2019
4. Oliver Burkeman, "Dirty secret: why is there still a housework gender gap?", *The Guardian*, 17 February 2018

what I'd call a staggering change. It seems to be the case that a woman's job is to work *and* look after the home and family. Just 2% of couples have taken shared parental leave since its introduction – another indication of social norms failing to change significantly.

Ironically – and disappointingly – women *and* men think their household contributions are unfair: 37% of men say they do less than their fair share at home despite both partners working. Women take on the mental load of family responsibility – they're the carers, feeders, shoppers, domestic managers and personal assistants, remembering appointments and birthdays, worrying about their families and planning how to get everyone where they need to be, fed and back again.[5] This, by the way, happens even before women have children and simply intensifies once kids' schedules are thrown into the mix. The housework gender gap pretty much stopped closing in the 1980s.[6]

Choosing identities

It's fairly widely acknowledged that "having it all" – juggling the perfect work-life balance, moving deftly from yummy mummy one minute to career girl the next – is a myth. Those descriptions themselves are part of the problem. We still seem to be in a Barbie-fuelled fantasy world where girls slip into different identities like outfits, depending on what it is that they're supposed to be doing at that moment, with the accompanying stylish set of expectations alongside the right shoes and handbag.

Girls' identities are troublingly narrow. Think about your school, your classroom, and the female identities on display there. In particular, think about the "good girl". The one who is always handing out the books or lending a pen. The one asked to show visitors around, or to befriend the new student, or to mentor the classmate who's not doing quite so well. The one sat next to the student who doesn't get it, or to the classmate who needs someone they won't be tempted to chat to, or with the disruptive

5. Emma, "The gender wars of household chores: a feminist comic", *The Guardian,* 26 May 2017

6. Oliver Burkeman, "Dirty secret: why is there still a housework gender gap?", *The Guardian,* 17 February 2018

boys as a calming influence. The girl who just gets on and does well. She is rarely rewarded for this behaviour. She's less likely to get "star of the week" or achievement certificates. After all, she's just like that, isn't she? It's who she is, it's not an effort. And she gets decent grades at the end of her five or seven years, and surely she's satisfied with that, isn't she?

These girls fulfil every expectation put upon them, and these expectations are deeply gendered. The "good girl" is probably not like that elsewhere, or wishes she wasn't. Most women I know are familiar with the dual-identity problem: with a few people – sometimes a *very* few – they feel they can be authentically themselves, but to function out there, in the world, they feel they have to be a little bit less than themselves in order to "fit in" and please others. The sociologist Diane Reay describes the Nice Girl, one of four feminine identities she observed in a primary school. These identities are shaped by parents, the media and society, but education has a significant role to play in their creation – or, hopefully, destruction.

In their book *Boys Don't Try?*, Matt Pinkett and Mark Roberts say "education is a subversive act".[7] At its heart, education's core purpose should be to enable young people to shape the identities of their future selves; to provide them with the knowledge, experience and belief that they are entitled to a fair and equal place in the world. For girls, this might still be the most subversive act of all. As the teacher Ben Newmark puts it on his blog, education should empower students to feel entitled "in the most proper, fair sense. Entitled to respect. Entitled to attention. Entitled to proper healthcare. Entitled to a place at an opera house, concert, museum or exhibition should they choose to go. Entitled to laws that protect them at work and entitled to pensions for a dignified old age regardless of their station in life."[8] And entitled to all this regardless of their gender. Because although modern feminism takes this as its minimum expectation, it's still far from the lived experiences of many girls and women.

---

7. Matt Pinkett and Mark Roberts, *Boys Don't Try? Rethinking masculinity in schools*, Routledge, 2019

8. Ben Newmark, "The point of it all", 20 July 2018, tinyurl.com/t75t9he

Polarising stereotypes

This isn't to say that men and boys don't feel this weight, too. Pinkett and Roberts do a thorough job of deconstructing alpha-masculinity and their call for a "tender masculinity"[9] resonates. But the gender gap seems to be widening even further when it comes to these masculine and feminine stereotypes. A quick look in any supermarket clothing section will tell you that boys are adventurous, exciting and interested in mechanics, dinosaurs and space, while girls like sparkly pink unicorns and should be kind. It's too easy to get distracted by the clothing debate and simply argue for unisex shelving.

Really, it's the significance of the messages that are being conveyed here. Slogans on girls' clothes tell them to be kind, happy and cheerful – to smile. Boys' slogans include "Future inventor", "One to watch", "Born to be wild" and "I'm just here to level up".[10] These slogans represent the way in which gender continues to be polarised, and it takes strong children – and parents – to counter that message. The sparkly pink unicorns are insidious, symptomatic of the infantilisation of females and of the hyper-femininity that seems to have gradually become the only brand of femininity we experience. Boys' clothes deal solely in reality, girls' in fantasy.[11] Girls' clothing is cut differently from toddlerhood, with some brands creating a disturbing sexualised divide even at this age – girls' shorts, for example, are often tighter, shorter, more fitted and lacking the pockets that boys take for granted.

Pockets are an interesting feminist point. Many women go mad for pockets because they're pretty unusual in dresses and skirts. As Barbara Burman and Ariane Fennetaux write in their book *The Pocket*, pockets create a physical space for privacy and personal possessions, things women historically lack, along with the ability to carry items like money

---

9.   Matt Pinkett and Mark Roberts, *Boys Don't Try? Rethinking masculinity in schools*, Routledge, 2019

10. Let Clothes Be Clothes campaign, letclothesbeclothes.co.uk

11. Let's clarify: unicorns are fun, and a playful interest in fantasy and imagination is great. But it's less great when it's the only option on the table

and keys, which grant independence.[12] They also affect the streamlined nature of women's clothing, making the body more bulky, less slim.

A glance at Lego's advertising from the 1970s shows boys and girls dressed in jeans and multicoloured jumpers, proudly holding their creations. There's very little difference between them, and the language is about imagination and creativity. Today, the Lego Friends sets are often bright pink; they include a hair-dressing salon, a baking competition and different mini-figures to those in the Lego City sets. It is Lego for girls, which sends out the message that the rest of it isn't.

There's nothing wrong with pink or blue. There's nothing wrong with glitter, sparkles, trucks, tutus, dinosaurs or being kind. There *is* something wrong with the deliberate reduction of femininity and masculinity to very narrow parameters that leave children without choice and girls feeling like they have to put everyone else first or they're not "being good". The middle ground is important – and it is being lost.

Girls and anxiety

Young women are suffering under the weight of all this expectation. Their mental health is in crisis, according to the Mental Health Foundation and a host of other studies. Women are more likely than men to experience eating disorders, depression, anxiety and to self-harm.[13] Studies exploring mental health and wellbeing among secondary pupils show that from Year 7 onwards, girls' happiness and self-worth declines. Nearly one in four teenage girls are likely to have self-harmed (more than twice as many as boys) and they generally report significantly lower levels of happiness, in almost every aspect of their lives.[14] Yet the conversational focus on resilience and self-care seems to once again place the responsibility on girls to "toughen up", rather than on society to change. It seems that as long as girls continue to perform academically, they are fine.

---

12. Barbara Burman and Ariane Fennetaux, *The Pocket: a hidden history of women's lives, 1660–1900,* Yale University Press, 2019

13. "Government makes women's mental health a top priority", Department of Health and Social Care, 20 December 2018

14. *The Good Childhood Report 2018: summary,* The Children's Society, 2018

They are not fine. Even though 70% of young women say they know online portrayals of success are unrealistic and don't tell the whole story,[15] they frequently don't *feel* that way and who can blame them? The barrage of expectation is overwhelming and, significantly, increasingly contradictory; the result is that women don't know where to turn. Traditionally "feminine" values – compassion, empathy, collaboration, listening, nurturing – have been sidelined in society in favour of traditionally "masculine" ones like aggression, competition and arrogance masquerading as self-confidence (see: every *Apprentice* participant). This perpetuates the myth that to "get ahead" you have to be willing to destroy the people around you. Girls are falling victim to the social message that to be successful, you have to become more "masculine", whether in work or relationships. Reclaiming the words "bitch" and "slut" doesn't mean that independently minded and sexually confident women are socially accepted, just that women are accepting the idea that "feminine" means passive, quiet and compliant. Changing the social narrative around what it means to be feminine or masculine is critical to create a happier and kinder society where all can benefit.

Masculine and/or feminine?

Of course, all men don't possess all-masculine characteristics, and all women aren't paragons of angelic femininity. But certain qualities have been ascribed to "masculine" and "feminine", with this binary being used to dictate the "work-life balance" of public and domestic. Historically, feminine and masculine identities seem to move in waves, pulling further apart and then drawing closer together again, but they never quite cross over.

Contemporary society – including the education system – continues to feed the narrative that masculine qualities are more desirable in the world of work and feminine qualities in the world at home. These views have hardened into virtual fact, despite new science regularly challenging them and ascribing them more to the patriarchal bias of scientific research.

15. *The Prince's Trust Macquarie Youth Index 2017,* The Prince's Trust, 2017

And these work-sphere masculine characteristics don't seem to be doing our society much good, do they? With rising levels of hate crime and domestic violence, and a UN report that calls child poverty in Britain "a social calamity and an economic disaster",[16] it seems that individualism and competition have done little to raise us all up. It can sometimes feel like we have a long way to go.

It's time to act

The good news – and there is plenty! – is that things *can* be improved for the girls and boys in our care. Education must face up to its social responsibilities and help to write a new narrative, by encouraging young people to see beyond the contemporary patriarchal messages that damage us all. For this book, I have identified four strands of action by which we can build a feminist education.

First, we need to recognise our part as educators in maintaining or reflecting cultural expectations. Our curricular choices are vital, ensuring that we challenge and critique the representation and diversity in our curriculum. Our day-to-day conversations, our textbooks and our role models all need to actively demonstrate the value of women to society in a wide range of roles and positions.

Second, we must model a genuine appreciation of all the traditionally feminine qualities, as well as the traditionally masculine. This is, in many ways, the most challenging of all. Even the divide of academic and pastoral echoes the traditional feminine/masculine binary – pastoral systems are nurturing, compassionate and collaborative, while the academic is more ambitious, rigorous and challenging. Schools are institutionally driven to privilege this academic, masculine side. How powerful it would be if we could add more compassion into the learning process, and more ambition into the pastoral.

Third, through our whole-school approach we can address gender consciously and thoughtfully. We all have unconscious biases – it's

---

16. Philip Alston, *Report of the Special Rapporteur on extreme poverty and human rights on his visit to the United Kingdom of Great Britain and Northern Ireland*, UN General Assembly, 23 April 2019

how aware of them we are and what we do to redress them that matter most. Our commitment to real equality and self-identity can be evident in every aspect of our schools, from seating plans to uniforms to the language we use, and to the ways in which we recognise students for achievement and behaviour.

Finally, and most critically, we need to empower young women with the self-confidence and security to shape their own identities. We need to remove the pressure of performance in their daily lives. We need to encourage them to share what they want and have the ambition to achieve it, whether it's becoming CEO of a FTSE 100 company, or being a great childminder, or developing an early-stage career that enables them to take time off to raise pre-school children. They need access to genuine leadership options. They need to be able to learn how to speak out, speak up and say what they want, whether it's negotiating a better salary or telling a partner it's his turn to look after their children. Boys, too, need to be encouraged to have these conversations – to say that, actually, they'd like to take some leave or work part-time or volunteer, without being made to feel like a freakish hero or a strange outsider.

Female voices are being heard more than ever, but there are also spaces where they are being suppressed more than ever, particularly when they speak about things other than "women's issues". By that, I mean family, relationships, children – things that are vitally important but have been pushed into a small box labelled "women" and put to one side as though they don't matter. *Everything* is a woman's issue. Women are 50% of the world's population. Globally, when girls are educated and equality increases, everything improves. The UN estimates that if all women had a primary education:

- Maternal deaths would reduce by two-thirds.
- There would be 15% fewer child deaths.
- 1.7 million fewer children would be malnourished.
- 14% fewer child marriages would take place.[17]

17. *Girls' Education: the facts*, UNESCO, October 2013

In the UK, we're fortunate that our young people don't have such crippling experiences. But that doesn't mean equality has been achieved. True feminism is about every girl and boy being able to decide for themselves how to express their identity and what role they wish to create for themselves in the world. A feminist education helps them to explore, experiment and learn how to be themselves – and how to achieve their own individual aspirations. It enables all students to feel entitled to an equal stake in society and the world. To do that, we have to teach them how they can make society more equal. As the writer and feminist activist Gloria Steinem has said, "It's not about integrating into a not-so-good system. It's about transforming it and making it better. If women have to acquire all the characteristics of a corporate world, it's probably not worth it."[18]

Wouldn't it be better for all of us if our society, at home and at work, included a little more compassion and empathy, a little more cooperation, a little less competition, and a lot more understanding and acceptance of the multiplicity of personal gender identities? What is required is a revolution in gender expectations, and there is no better place to start than in our schools.

---

18. Laura Kray, Jessica Kennedy and Gillian Ku, "Are women more ethical than men?", *Greater Good Magazine*, Greater Good Science Center at the University of California, Berkeley, 8 March 2017

A word on language

In this book, there are some words I have deliberately chosen to use. I have tended to use "anxious" or "anxiousness" rather than "anxiety", with the intention of describing a more general sense of unease or discomfort. "Anxiety" has taken on a more medicalised meaning, with students "having anxiety" or "suffering anxiety" as an illness. Although there is a range of severity when it comes to anxiousness, for the most part I am discussing the general feeling, rather than something that might need intervention from a medical professional.

I have also tried to use the phrase "mental fitness". I feel that "mental health" is often used interchangeably with "mental ill health" and I'm referring more to a general improvement in wellbeing and fitness, rather than a condition that might require support from child and adolescent mental health services (CAMHS) or a GP. "Mental fitness" is also distinct from "mental illness", which, for me, is more about the kinds of conditions that require medication or focused talking therapies. The use of language is ever-changing in this area, so I have used what feels right now.

As stated in the introduction, I have used "feminine" and "masculine" to discuss the traditionally ascribed characteristics of gender. I have also borrowed some definitions from the US organisation Gender Spectrum: "gender identity" refers to our own core concept of self, as masculine, feminine or a blend of both; "gender expression" refers to how we communicate our gender to others, e.g. through clothing, hairstyles and mannerisms. According to Gender Spectrum, "Expression is distinct from identity – we can't assume a person's gender identity based on their gender expression. For example, a boy may like to wear skirts or dresses. His choice in clothing doesn't define his gender identity; it simply means that he prefers (at least some of the time) to wear clothes that society has typically associated with girls."[19]

19. "Understanding gender", genderspectrum.org, accessed 2019

Part I

The origins of expectation

History, despite its wrenching pain, cannot be unlived, but if faced with courage, need not be lived again – **Maya Angelou**

In **Part I: The origins of expectation**, I will explore the sources of some deeply held beliefs about gender. And I will argue that some of the "unassailable" facts of biological thinking are not quite as clear-cut as they might seem.

So many of our gender assumptions are claimed to be rooted in biology. We are told that boys' need to "show off" is connected to the evolutionary imperative to find a mate, and that girls' "need" to play with dolls is evidence of the "natural" nurturing instinct of women (as though they hadn't been led by the hand to the pink aisle and asked to pick something). To accept this narrative is to tell children that in order to move beyond traditional gender expectations, they will have to fight against their natural instincts. If that were true, it would be incredibly difficult to do so and would potentially cause some of the anxieties that young people experience around gender. Instead, I believe that gender is highly socialised and that our scientific understanding of gender is constantly changing.

We need to consciously address the flaws in beliefs about gender, which can be so entrenched that they *feel* natural – but they can be challenged in a way that benefits us all.

1. Biological difference

There is no female mind. The brain is not an organ of sex. One may as well speak of a female liver – Charlotte Perkins Gilman

I sometimes try to imagine what would have happened if we'd known the bonobo first and the chimpanzee only later – or not at all. The discussion about human evolution might not revolve as much around violence, warfare and male dominance, but rather around sexuality, empathy, caring and cooperation. What a different intellectual landscape we would occupy! – Frans de Waal, *Our Inner Ape: A Leading Primatologist Explains Why We Are Who We Are*

A lot of biological science is dedicated to gender difference – trying to understand our evolutionary past and map this on to our future. Maybe we don't need to change our gendered expectations if there are scientific reasons for them. It's not our fault! It's biology!

The thing is, that doesn't seem to be true. There are biological differences in women's and men's reproductive organs and some hormones. But, mostly, there's more physical difference *within* the sexes than *between* them. Although men are, on average, about six inches taller and have double the upper-body strength of women, those averages mask a huge range.[20] Anybody watching sportswomen at the top of their game couldn't sustain an argument that they aren't fitter, stronger and healthier than most women *and* men on an average day. Logically, this all makes complete sense. Yet we're mired in these physical expectations, which have an impact on career aspirations.

Construction, for example, has the lowest gender diversity of any industry, at just 13%.[21] Women in construction are typically found in offices and in design, rather than literally doing the heavy lifting: in 2006, just five of the 10,000 people working on Wembley Stadium's construction were women.[22] Discussions about girls' physiology tend to assert their weakness, as though all men are bodybuilders and women can't put on muscle. But if the attributes of physical speed, strength and muscle mass were purely down to gender, we would expect to see some global parity – men across the world of similar height, weight, strength and build. Instead, we see huge variation. Women in England are, on average, 161cm tall – the same as an average Indian man. While the mean average height of men in a country is always higher than the mean average height of women, the differences are pretty small.[23]

Angela Saini's book *Inferior* explains that women's bodies are stronger and more robust than men's – women die later and recover from illness more quickly. Yet, she says, "the fact that [mortality rates are] not even equal, but are skewed in favour of boys, means that girls' natural power to survive is being forcibly degraded by the societies they are born into".[24] Even the fact that women get sicker more often could, Saini argues, be a result of their more powerful immune systems, but it's

20. Angela Saini, *Inferior: how science got women wrong – and the new research that's rewriting the story*, HarperCollins, 2017

21. *Inspiring Change: attracting women into construction*, Balfour Beatty, October 2017

22. Julie Bindel, "Can she fix it?", *The Guardian*, 14 August 2006

23. "Average human height by country", Wikipedia, tinyurl.com/qq2tkpe, accessed 2019. This data also shows differences between each country in the UK – so social background has a significant role to play beyond the pure biology of gender

24. Angela Saini, *Inferior: how science got women wrong – and the new research that's rewriting the story*, HarperCollins, 2017

impossible to say for sure because there is so little research into gender as a factor in illness and life expectancy. Indeed, much scientific research has a decidedly male bias: Caroline Criado Perez explores just how much in her book *Invisible Women*,[25] which includes nuggets of information like the fact that crash test dummies are based on men, so women are 47% more likely to be seriously injured in a car crash. Women's heart attack symptoms are completely different, so the well-publicised chest and arm pains don't act as a warning sign to women. And mobile phones and house bricks are built for male hands. Research is conducted based on male averages, rather than the whole population.

Evolutionary explanations

Expectations of men and women often have an evolutionary connection, linked to reproductive need. Consider the "alpha male" myth. Typical representations of "toxic" masculinity centre on this alpha male: he must be aggressive, strong, powerful, controlling and dominant, to prove his reproductive value to potential mates. He must have sex with as many women as possible to spread his precious seed, and cannot be expected to be monogamous. He shows off his power like a peacock displays his tail, via showy cars, gifts or other physical symbols of his status and wealth. The more powerful and aggressive, the more likely he is to find a sexual partner.

Women, on the other hand? Passive recipients of said seed, they shouldn't enjoy sex (no evolutionary need for that) and should stay looking young and attractive so men know they are good fertile stock. They should focus on nurturing, preferably raising children, but if that's not possible they should exhibit this love and care in whatever way they can. When it comes to sex, they should be as choosy and selective as possible (definitely not promiscuous) to select the best mate.

It's disturbing how much of the gender narrative still mimics this crude evolutionary explanation, much of which comes from several key theories or experiments. In 1948, for example, the biologist Angus Bateman put together male and female fruit flies with different mutations

---

25. Caroline Criado Perez, *Invisible Women: exposing data bias in a world designed for men*, Penguin, 2019

and watched for the offspring, using the mutations to tell which offspring belonged to which flies. According to his observations, the female flies regularly rejected the males; he concluded that this was evidence for the evolutionary theory of sexual selection and competition, extrapolating this to humans.[26] Bateman's work wasn't widely published until the 1970s, when the biologist Robert Trivers picked it up; since then it's been cited 11,000 times, despite never being replicated.

In her book *Testosterone Rex*, Cordelia Fine points out several problems with the data, including the fact that Bateman's observations were visual, based on transmission of mutation (so there's doubt over parentage) and didn't take into account when the offspring died. When published, the data was split in two: half of it (the publicised half) suggested male promiscuity; half of it suggested *female* promiscuity.[27] Neither promiscuity nor competition were shown to be solely male traits, but were actually evenly split. Similar studies of insect and mammalian reproduction have suggested the same male-focused sexual selection, but this has been extrapolated to explain human Western patriarchal cultures, taking quite a leap. More recent research instead recognises that human sexuality is far, far more complex and multifaceted. Rather than being driven by evolutionary instinct, according to Gillian R Brown et al, "factors such as sex-biased mortality, sex-ratio, population density and variation in mate quality, are likely to impact mating behaviour in humans".[28] The gendered narrative of men needing to prove their value to choosy females simply doesn't hold up.

Evolutionary biology also plays a part in the narrative of gender roles in human society, or at least in Western human society. Men are hunters, while women are described, often quite dismissively,

26. Gillian R Brown, Kevin N Laland and Monique Borgerhoff Mulder, "Bateman's principles and human sex roles", *Trends in Ecology and Evolution*, 24:6–14, June 2009

27. Cordelia Fine, *Testosterone Rex*, Icon Books, 2017. Fine and Saini both explore Darwin's response to female scientists questioning his conclusions, and argue that his scientific hypotheses are significantly influenced by his own society's rules around gender

28. Gillian R Brown, Kevin N Laland and Monique Borgerhoff Mulder, "Bateman's principles and human sex roles", *Trends in Ecology and Evolution*, 24:6–14, June 2009

as gatherers (collecting plant foods and rearing small game while looking after children and the home). Fine argues that much of this is theoretical and ultimately unknowable. She cites studies positing that female gatherers could have brought home two-thirds of a family's food, saving them from starvation. She also presents anthropological research of tribes relatively untouched by modernity, where women hunt, are stronger and faster than men, and either carry their children with them or adopt a shared-parenting model so they can hunt alone.[29] Other studies contradict the evidence base for the hunter-gatherer theory: the anthropologist Adrienne Zihlman, for example, has suggested that women's hunting was likely done with digging sticks, multifunctional tools used to gather plants and kill small animals, but because these tools would have been wooden and therefore degradable, there are no fossilised traces, unlike the stone tools that anthropologists assume were used for hunting bigger animals.[30] This argument, coupled with the importance Zihlman places on female hunting as essential for survival, positions women quite differently.

Flawed arguments

Why is all this relevant in a book about education? The answer is that these theories have permeated our society and been used as the rationale for traditional gender roles – and if the science is flawed, so is the justification. If Victorian scientists were influenced by their own patriarchal society to suggest biased, flawed hypotheses, then by accepting their theories and continuing to use them as justification for male and female behaviour, we are endorsing not the science but the gendered social divide the scientists lived in.

Students should be made aware of the flaws in this thinking, as well as our own unconscious biases. Socialisation plays a much more significant part in gender-role creation than biology, despite evolutionary claims (and specious arguments about masculine strength and feminine

29. Cordelia Fine, *Testosterone Rex,* Icon Books, 2017

30. Adrienne L Zihlman, "The real females of human evolution", *Evolutionary Anthropology,* 21:6, 19 December 2012

passivity) being used to justify the status quo. Challenging these theories has significant implications, not only for attitudes towards sex and sexuality, but also for expectations surrounding parenting, family and work – and those domains, in particular, are where the gender stereotypes begin to become damaging.

The evolutionary argument isn't a one-size-fits-all rule. Among animals, there are almost as many models of reproduction and parenting as there are species. Animals have families where females collectively look after the young, or males do; where females have one, two or more partners; where males are monogamous or polygamous; where creatures mate for life or in a single encounter. It's the same in human societies. Anthropologists have charted a variety of family and gender patterns, of virtually every combination. It seems bizarre to characterise the Western stereotypes as "natural", as though they are the only way to behave. Not only does that ignore much research on animals and humans, but it also fails to acknowledge the role of the social, cultural, economic and political pressures that are brought to bear on individuals, female and male, when establishing their gender roles and their families.

Male and female brains

Here are some familiar statements: men are better at reading maps; women are better at communicating; men use the side of the brain that controls linear thinking, sequencing and spatial skills; women use the side controlling creativity and imagination. Doesn't it make logical sense that boys prefer some subjects while girls are better at others? That some activities help girls to learn, while a different approach is needed if we want boys to succeed?

The research problem is that it's virtually impossible to distinguish between biology and socialisation. Just as with height, weight and strength, there is a huge variety. And it's difficult to find a human brain that can be interpreted *without* social expectation already having made an impact. One of the most significant studies arguing for the existence of "male" and "female" brains comes from Simon Baron-Cohen, a psychologist and neuroscientist. Baron-Cohen wanted to see whether sex hormones delivered in the womb created female empathisers or male systemisers, so he studied 100 babies less than two days old. A large proportion showed no preference, while 40% of boys preferred the mechanical mobile they were shown and 36% of girls preferred a picture of a face. Yet, in his 2003 book *The Essential Difference*, Baron-Cohen argues that this study demonstrated a conclusive sex difference between males and females from birth. He suggests that this is responsible for, among other things, men's and women's hobbies:

> *"Those with the male brain tend to spend hours happily engaged in car or motorbike maintenance, small-plane piloting, sailing, bird- or train-spotting, mathematics, tweaking their sound systems, or busy with computer games and programming, DIY or photography. Those with the female brain tend to prefer to spend their time engaged in coffee mornings or having supper with friends, advising them on relationship problems, or caring for people or pets, or working for volunteer phone-lines listening to depressed, hurt, needy or even suicidal callers."*[31]

The list is peculiar, in that it's almost ridiculously narrow in its cultural bias, as well as seeming to suggest that male brains are more suited to the complex and well-remunerated work of computing and mathematics, while female brains are more suited to nurturing, which coincidentally is much less well-rewarded by society. Baron-Cohen ignores the many people performing jobs very successfully in the "wrong" gender, as well as the significant role of socialisation. In the not-so-distant past, for example, women were the dominant gender in computing.[32]

Baron-Cohen's experiment hasn't been replicated (a red flag as far as scientific reliability is concerned), but it has been cited in other studies

---

31. Simon Baron-Cohen, *The Essential Difference: men, women and the extreme male brain*, Penguin, 2004

32. Marie Hicks, "Women's work: how Britain discarded its female computer programmers", *New Statesman*, 1 February 2019

and received widespread media attention in which it was held up as proof that gender is in the brain. There was also evidence of social gendering in the maternity ward – Baron-Cohen's assistant described the pink and blue balloons and cards surrounding the babies being observed. Studies into toy preferences have shown that they don't truly develop until the ages of one and two, when children have had months of gender-specific toys, books and even language, with adults using different endearments for girls and boys. Before babies can become truly, consciously aware of anything around them, they're being nudged into a gendered experience of the world.

Sexism in science: the patriarchy problem

Angela Saini and Cordelia Fine – and the many studies they review and scientists they interview, male and female – agree that science can be sexist. Scientists are fallible, like everyone else, and just as socialised. Meanwhile, the media picks up sexy, interesting stories, reporting them as quickly as possible, reducing ideas to key facts without explanation. And it's not just the news media, either: Robert Trivers' write-up of Bateman's research was also covered in a feature in *Playboy* (August 1978) under the headline "Do men need to cheat on their women? A new science says yes". A quick Google search reveals similar headlines in multiple media, repeated regularly over the past 40 years, and they pretty much all use Bateman's study as justification for socially unacceptable behaviour like cheating on a partner. Of course, they conveniently assume that women don't cheat.

Is there sexism in Saini and Fine's books? Perhaps – they're open about their pursuit of a feminist agenda. But they are equally clear that the science they examine at least casts doubt on the veracity of certain theories. When there are studies arguing both sides, we can at least interrogate them critically before we agree with either one entirely.

Sexism in science is just one facet of social conditioning into a patriarchal system that encourages a black and white understanding of the flexibility of gender identities: the "masculine" and "feminine" as contrasting sets of values and attributes. It's important that teachers and school leaders understand this sexism and how its presentation as fact can imprison young women and men in socially prescribed roles. The Western view of gender is hardly the norm worldwide, which itself casts doubt on the biological narrative. As suggested by Professor John Dupré, a philosopher of science, accepting this evolutionary idea means there's no need to change anything when it comes to equality:

> *"If status-seeking is shown to be an adaptation for male reproductive success, we have finally located the biological reason for the much lower status achieved by women. Let's leave the men to pursue status while the women devote themselves to the important business of staying young."*[33]

Challenging this narrative has positive implications for men as well as women. If young women can be freed from the need to perpetually present themselves as youthful, passive and willing (but choosy) when it comes to sex, we can also eliminate the idea that young men are always looking for their next opportunity for sexual reproduction, without the same capacity as women for love, commitment or partnership in parenting.

33. John Dupré, "Scientism, sexism and sociobiology: one more link in the chain", *Behavioral and Brain Sciences*, 16:2, 1993

2. Socialisation and performance of gender roles

If women are expected to do the same work as men,
we must teach them the same things – Plato

Much of being a teenager is about shaping your future identity. It's a series of choices – from music, reading and sports to how you dress and what your opinions are – and these are often made in opposition to something else or to align with someone else.

The construction of identity is a lifelong process, but gaining a strong sense of who we are in our teenage years can provide a feeling of purpose and belonging as we enter adult life. Not only does this build confidence and self-esteem, but it also acts as a buffer, a sort of inoculation against difficult situations. In the 1950s, the sociologist Erving Goffman wrote about identity being created through social expectations: we understand, implicitly or explicitly, the views of others, and then decide how far we take them into ourselves and develop them as values or controlling factors. These norms and values become so embedded that we believe them to be "natural".[34]

---

34. Erving Goffman, *The Presentation of Self in Everyday Life,* Anchor, 1959

The philosopher Judith Butler specifically applies this to gender norms: from a foetus's 20-week scan, expectations associated with gender are attached to every facet of that child's life.[35] Most contemporary discussion acknowledges the role that socialisation plays in shaping gender identity, and the fact that this begins to happen incredibly early. We know that any skill or trait, carefully nurtured, encouraged and praised, will develop in time. In some ways, gender identity is like learning to read, play the piano or ride a bike: when we're taught to behave in a certain way, praised when we do and criticised when we don't, it becomes part of us to want to fit into that ideal. The difference is that when we play the piano instead of climbing mountains, it's not particularly harmful, unlike some aspects of gendered roles.

We all have the capacity to express feminine and masculine traits to a greater or lesser extent. The question is how far girls and boys are being socialised into a binary, rather than being encouraged to acknowledge and explore all aspects of themselves. Words like bigender, agender and genderfluid represent a search for a way out of this binary. There have always been people operating outside the binary, but in some ways gender identities are being pushed further and further apart.

Nurture more than nature

In Darwin's *The Descent of Man*, he introduced the idea of sexual selection and described the   physical qualities that men and women "needed" to successfully reproduce, as well as the emotional and mental qualities. He claimed that men were naturally superior:

> "If two lists were made of the most eminent men and women in poetry, painting, sculpture, music — comprising composition and performance, history, science, and philosophy, with half-a-dozen names under each subject, the two lists would not bear comparison."[36]

35. Judith Butler, *Undoing Gender*, Routledge, 2004
36. Charles Darwin, *The Descent of Man, and Selection in Relation to Sex*, John Murray, 1871

However, rather than simply accepting male dominance in art, culture and science, as Darwin did, we've been acknowledging for some time that the apparent lack of female contributions is far more complex. At its heart is the fact that many women weren't educated or encouraged in the ways that men were; they weren't given the creative freedom, ambition, knowledge and opportunity to be productive in the same way. For centuries, women who achieved success in these male-dominated spheres were considered odd or unnatural, rather than celebrated. And so, the lists of "eminent men and women" are borne of society, not biology.

Girls and women have been expected to spend their time nurturing others and making themselves look attractive primarily for the pleasure of others. They have been encouraged to support other people, not to follow the ambition that is often needed to become "eminent" (which also involves the confidence to enter the public space, rather than remaining private and domestic). Every year, the Children's Society surveys children's attitudes, finding that this still holds broadly true.[37] Children are more likely to say a girl's most important qualities are "being good-looking" and "being caring". For boys, being good-looking is also considered important, but less so than "being tough" and "being funny". The children who believed these stereotypes were less happy than those who didn't. When girls found comments about people's appearance or sexuality were common, their wellbeing declined. It seems that enacting those roles only makes girls and boys more and more unhappy. Perhaps this is because of the conflict that exists between their own self-identity and the gendered binary they feel they must perform.

The good girl at school

A lot of educational research into gender is boy-focused. Even studies that include girls often end up focusing on boys because of their perceived underachievement, underperformance or worse behaviour. Girls become a comparison point, a lens through which we understand how boys work.

---

37. *The Good Childhood Report 2018: summary*, The Children's Society, 2018

Girls feel this themselves, reporting that they only become the focus of conversation when teenage pregnancy is an issue.[38]

According to girls and their teachers, girls are more motivated than their male counterparts. In studies, they demonstrate positive adaptive behaviours including:[39]

- Being able to plan work independently.
- Good task management in class and at home.
- Effective organisation of study time and materials.
- Willingness to persist with challenging materials.[40]
- Willingness to persist even when a task is boring.[41]

The "good girl" is well-behaved, on-task, does what she's asked and generally "gets on". Often, she even helps the person next to her, either academically or as seating-plan inoculation against male disruption.

There are, though, some traits that could hold her back. Friendships can be difficult because other students see her as clever, sensible and a "contaminating presence"[42] who is boring and prevents fun. She's also self-surveilling and hypercritical of herself, certainly more prone to

38. Susan Jones and Debra Myhill, "'Troublesome Boys' and 'Compliant Girls': gender identity and perceptions of achievement and underachievement", *British Journal of Sociology of Education*, 25:5, November 2004

39. Myfanwy Bugler, Sarah P McGeown and Helen St Clair-Thompson, "Gender differences in adolescents' academic motivation and classroom behaviour", *Educational Psychology*, 35:5, 2013

40. Mary Ainley, Kylie Hillman and Suzanne Hidi, "Gender and interest processes in response to literary texts: situational and individual interest", *Learning and Instruction*, 12:4, 2002

41. Marion Williams, Robert Burden and Ursula Lanvers, "'French is the language of love and stuff': student perceptions of issues related to motivation in learning a foreign language", *British Educational Research Journal*, 28:4, August 2002

42. Diane Reay, "'Spice Girls', 'Nice Girls', 'Girlies' and 'Tomboys': gender discourses, girls' cultures and femininities in the primary classroom", *Gender and Education*, 13:2, 2001

anxiousness and indecision.[43] Self-sabotage might be her biggest problem: when failure seems likely, she tends to decide it's best not to do the work at all, or she becomes so passive and reliant on someone else that it's not really her work any more.[44] Even when she's not doing her work, this girl is less likely to get into trouble because her actions are excused as "lack of confidence".

Performing the good girl

These are external behaviours. They're part of the performance of being the good girl and obeying the social requirements of feminine behaviour. Yet they also act as a mask, hiding where girls do need support or challenge. According to a study by Nicola Rollock, for example, black girls "recognise the status" of good uniform, good behaviour and positive interactions. Yet, Rollock points out, black girls might do well academically compared with black boys, but not particularly compared with white girls.[45] She argues that by accepting the compliance required of them, they miss out. They go under the radar when it comes to increasing their cultural capital, diagnosing their academic needs, challenging their aspiration, or supporting their motivation. In a busy classroom, it's all too easy to pay attention to the students who demand it, rather than those who need it.

Research frequently describes girls' behaviour relatively positively in terms of classroom management:

> "It may be that girls are, in general, more conscientious, compliant or self-disciplined, and therefore less likely to allow their motivation to influence negative classroom

43. Myfanwy Bugler, Sarah P McGeown and Helen St Clair-Thompson, "Gender differences in adolescents' academic motivation and classroom behaviour", *Educational Psychology*, 35:5, 2013

44. Susan Jones and Debra Myhill, "'Troublesome Boys' and 'Compliant Girls': gender identity and perceptions of achievement and underachievement", *British Journal of Sociology of Education* 25:5, November 2004

45. In 2006, for example, 7.4% more white girls achieved five or more A*–C grades than black girls

behaviours. In other words, even in classroom situations in which girls are unmotivated, their personalities make them less likely to actively display negative behaviours.[46]

However, these qualities are of questionable benefit outside school, as Debra Myhill writes:

"This pattern of interaction behaviour raises two important questions. Firstly, does the behaviour of the high-achieving girl ultimately disadvantage them? Miller (1996) claims that these attributes of girls are often used to demean girls' achievements: girls' successes are understood to be the result of hard work rather than the 'brilliance' which boys are presumed to possess. … A further disadvantage that may ultimately befall compliant girls is that the very attributes which may advantage them in school with regard to examination success may disadvantage them in the workplace. Few company executives, politicians, lawyers and so on would be described as compliant and conformist, though their PAs may well be!"[47]

An alternative performance

Those girls who don't fit the "good girl" brand are also under-represented in research, but Diane Reay's 2001 primary school study explores three specific types, named by the girls themselves.[48]

Girlies are intensely active in maintaining conventional heterosexual relationships, "writing messages, flirting and discussing relationships". Described by others as "dumb" and "stupid", they

---

46. Myfanwy Bugler, Sarah P McGeown and Helen St Clair-Thompson, "Gender differences in adolescents' academic motivation and classroom behaviour", *Educational Psychology*, 35:5, 2013

47. Debra Myhill, "Bad boys and good girls? Patterns of interaction and response in whole class teaching", *British Educational Research Journal*, 28:3, 2002

48. Diane Reay, "'Spice Girls', 'Nice Girls', 'Girlies' and 'Tomboys': gender discourses, girls' cultures and femininities in the primary classroom", *Gender and Education*, 13:2, 2001

often mask their own ability in order to appear less threatening and avoid being labelled boring like the Nice Girls (similar to my "good girls"). Spice Girls overlap with the Girlies: they are keen to maintain heterosexual relationships, but they also deliberately manipulate social power and hierarchies. Most often, these identities fall back on the two pillars of appearance and sexuality: the classic "schoolgirl uniform in disarray" à la Britney Spears 1998, or the social-status-obsessed Plastics of *Mean Girls*, who use their bitchy communication skills to get ahead at the expense of others.

The Spice Girls aren't afraid to call out others, humiliate or embarrass – or support and laugh with – as long as it serves their social purpose. This, Reay suggests, goes hand in hand with a sexual knowingness cultivated largely to solidify this power; teachers often see the Spice Girls as "too assertive", "aggressive", "precocious" or "too knowing". They inhabit a difficult space, one in which they are trying to move beyond the conventions of the Girlies and the Nice Girls, but are proclaiming their sexuality and sexual knowledge – not exactly the stuff of feminist dreams and still intensely dependent on heteronormative values.

Finally, there are the Tomboys, the smallest of the groups in Reay's study. These girls look down on other girls, seeing them as less capable. In their way, they even more strongly confirm the gender binary: they almost refuse to see themselves as girls because they want to identify with a more masculine gender identity. Reay argues that even those girls attempting to transgress the feminine stereotypes fail: "girls' subversions are contained within and rarely challenge the existing structures."[49] They are, in short, performing a small variety of female roles prescribed for them by social expectation.

Beyond the academic

Reay's work might be 20 years old, but think of any class and you're likely to find girls fitting themselves into those categories. School life favours good

49. Diane Reay, "'Spice Girls', 'Nice Girls', 'Girlies' and 'Tomboys': gender discourses, girls' cultures and femininities in the primary classroom", *Gender and Education*, 13:2, 2001

girls: if you need someone to hand out the books, take a note to reception or mentor another student, it'll be a good girl you ask. But this can be damaging.

The weight of social expectation means girls are unable to explore themselves fully, both in school and out. They lack the confidence to demand something different to the opportunities on offer to them. Expectations of the good girl in particular breed perfectionism and anxiousness, because few can live up to those stifling standards without experiencing frustration and difficulty. And then we demand that they take risks and be resilient in exams as well. We're setting them up to fail in a game that is rigged. The other feminine identities on offer are just as limiting, and the covert – or not so covert – criticism of their behaviour, sexuality and ability leaves these girls in a hinterland between the boys and the good girls, where they seek to be a blend of masculine and feminine yet are perpetually made to feel that this is the wrong choice.

Schools are about the academic, for sure, but I don't know any teacher who would claim they are *solely* about the academic. And although girls are doing extremely well when it comes to grades and exams, they are being seriously let down by a system that privileges the good girl and criticises everyone else for failing to be like her. This system condemns the Spice Girls' bids for power, yet neglects to suggest that perhaps there are more effective – kinder and more collaborative – ways to gain social status. And it characterises girls who like sports as tom*boys*, rather than sporty girls. These expectations of girls are all too familiar: they are pervasive across society, not just in education, and they speak to the way that women are pushed to become passive and domestic, putting others before themselves.

This comes at incredible cost to their own self-esteem and robs them of opportunities. Chris Curtis, a head of English from Birmingham, reflected in a blog post on his own daughters' experiences at school:

> "My daughters are perfect 'Blue Peter' girls. They'd love to enter a competition. They'd love to save a hedgehog. They'd love to know about compost making. They just want to get involved. And, this is the other problem: 'the kind good girl type'. They get lumbered with everything.

Here's a new student. Meet the 'Blue Peter' girls. It became a joke in our house about how every new student, and I mean every new student, was paired up with my daughters when they arrived at school. Good girls were seen, and are often seen, as the problem solvers. We'll just use Jenny because she's kind and friendly. My daughters were that girl and they got fed up of it.[50]

I have no doubt that Chris's daughters want to be kind and friendly to others, and that is a fabulous quality everyone could exhibit a little more of. But they clearly also want to be involved with everything else, and perhaps those opportunities were given to someone who "needed to be engaged".

Along with the expectation of kindness and care and friendship, there is a counter-expectation, which is that good girls don't get angry. Or upset, or sad, or frustrated. When one in four girls are self-harming, as a way of "coping with extreme emotional distress",[51] is it time to ask if a part of that is because girls actually aren't allowed to express their emotions? The sociologist Patricia Adler describes self-harm as emotional self-help that enables people to release emotion, regain control and gain relief. She argues that "it's part of women's gender socialisation to turn inwards and self-destruct when they are upset. Men, when they are upset, tend to get angry; they externalise."[52] Back in the classroom, that refusal to exhibit anger or stress can sometimes simply manifest in refusal to do the work: if it's too challenging and creates frustration, then the anxiousness created by holding that emotion back means there's no room to do the work itself, and all those positive adaptive strategies go out the window. Sometimes, this does manifest in physical or emotional self-harm.

---

50. Chris Curtis, "Girls do try and that might be where the problem lies", *Learning From My Mistakes: an English teacher's blog*, 21 July 2019, tinyurl.com/tzcys4z

51. Patricia A Adler, *The Tender Cut: inside the hidden world of self-injury*, New York University Press, 2011

52. Ibid.

And even if girls aren't being driven to self-harm by the damaging conflict of gender expectations, they're certainly being held back. They're not being given the room and opportunity to explore other experiences, other identities, other choices.

The boys in the room

Boys benefit from an increased awareness of this conflict, too, not least because they are also struggling with their concept of self. They are pushed into the role of the alpha male, just as girls are directed into their nurturing roles. Recent research into children's literature, for example, explored the top 100 picture books of 2017.[53] It focused on the creatures being gendered and found that males were typically powerful, wild and dangerous (dragons, bears and tigers) while females were birds, cats and insects (small, vulnerable prey creatures). Male characters were almost always portrayed as the villain or demonstrated an aggressive brand of male dominance. Adult male carers were nearly invisible, with twice as many female teachers portrayed, while fathers were depicted alone in just four books – they were usually absent or accompanied by a co-parent. Eradicating this gender bias is just as beneficial to boys as it is to girls.

Our teenage years are vital to developing our sense of self, including our gender identity. Students need space and flexibility to explore and decide who they want to become. What do they need to be able to do that? How can we offer those opportunities?

Gender is learned. Even though this book is about girls, it's also about boys, who don't want to be tied into a particular version of masculine either. We need to incorporate a much wider range of feminine qualities into our daily experiences. And we need to reconfigure the understanding of gender, feminism and equality in secondary schools into something that includes a multiplicity of gender identities – or even none at all – in a quest to build a more compassionate, nurturing and altogether kinder society.

---

53. Donna Ferguson, "Must monsters always be male? Huge gender bias revealed in children's books", *The Guardian*, 21 January 2018

Part II

Exploring the curriculum

Teach her that the idea of 'gender roles' is absolute nonsense. Do not ever tell her that she should or should not do something because she is a girl. 'Because you are a girl' is never reason for anything. Ever – Chimamanda Ngozi Adichie, *Dear Ijeawele, or a Feminist Manifesto in Fifteen Suggestions*

The rest of this book is about what we can do in our day-to-day teaching practice to break down gender biases and stereotypes, in order to create an inclusive approach that builds girls' confidence in themselves and their gender. I suggest dipping in and out as you need to, depending on your role and interests.

In **Part II: Exploring the curriculum**, I start by taking a cross-curricular approach to extended writing and oracy. Then I look at the ways in which different subjects can explore gender through their content. I also discuss how gender affects motivation and take-up of different subjects.

In **Part III: The whole girl**, I explore different aspects of girlhood that schools can work to support. Each chapter includes a discussion of some of the major issues that could be addressed, along with practical suggestions and references to other organisations that can help.

Finally, in **Part IV: Modelling the feminist society**, I examine the way in which schools as institutions can model the society we want for our young people. Through our working practices with staff, attitudes to caring responsibilities and wellbeing, and provision of leadership models and experiences for girls, we can demonstrate a different approach to leadership.

3. Extended writing

Men have had every advantage of us in telling their own story. Education has been theirs in so much higher a degree; the pen has been in their hands – Jane Austen, *Persuasion*

Writing is essential not just for exam success, but also, in a feminist model, for giving women the ability to communicate clearly, with a range of audiences, and to know precisely what they want to say and how. In addition, writing is a great way to explore personal identity.

Research, to an extent, supports the stereotype that girls are better (and more enthusiastic) writers and readers than boys. Indeed, we seem to spend a lot of time thinking about how to get boys to read and write, and about which writers will best engage them. A report for the National Literacy Trust suggests that around 58% of girls "enjoy writing either very much or quite a lot", compared with 42% of boys. Girls are slightly more likely to write in their own time and for themselves, in a wider range of genres including fiction, journals, poems, letters, blogs or other online content. Enjoyment of writing is also moderately linked with enjoyment of reading. Unsurprisingly, those who write and read in their own time are more academically successful.[54]

---

54. Christina Clark and Anne Teravainen, *Writing for Enjoyment and its Link to Wider Writing*, National Literacy Trust, June 2017

Yet 58% isn't all girls by a long way. In my experience, younger girls entering secondary school are more likely to enjoy writing, finding it more difficult in later years. Perhaps this is because as they get older, the writing they do becomes more taxing, more associated with school, less experimental and less fun. At the same time, girls become more aware that creative writing in particular often demands that they give of themselves and reveal something personal, which can be tough. The highest quality academic writing – particularly at A level, but also in many GCSE essay subjects – asks that students offer their own opinions, arguments and evaluations in order to be successful. Writing is, at its heart, a revealing of self. Thus, in school you are offering yourself up to scrutiny, feedback and judgement – of course it's a challenge! And even more so for girls, who are constantly aware of the tension between doing as they're asked and meeting criteria, and the risk-taking and flair associated with the higher grades.

Although this section is mostly about school-based writing, let's take a diversion into the professional treatment of female writers. The very existence of "women's fiction" is a reminder of gender inequalities – is everything else, then, "men's fiction"? The label is usually applied to writing by women about families, domestic life or relationships. The novelist Sunni Overend points out that "women do not own stories of love and vulnerability, family and friendship, just as men do not own stories of violence, heroism and strength".[55] Yet when male writers explore families and the domestic sphere, their work is more likely to be labelled as literary fiction, or "state of the nation" fiction, or even just fiction. Female writers, meanwhile, get a floral cover, a woman's silhouette and a curly title font.

Women are also at a disadvantage when it comes to simply *getting* a professional writing job – just 16% of screenwriters in UK film are women, for example. Literary criticism tends to focus on male-written books, according to the US organisation VIDA: Women in Literary Arts,[56] which analyses the stats every year. VIDA has been challenged for

---

55. Sunni Overend, "Why Sunni Overend resents the term 'women's fiction'", HarperCollins blog, 3 January 2017, tinyurl.com/wsy3d4t
56. Amy King and Sarah Clark, *The 2017 VIDA Count,* VIDA: Women in Literary Arts

only counting reviews that appear in print; its response is that discussion of the work of women and minorities is being confined to online spaces, which usually have a less dedicated readership and lack the intellectual prestige of print publications. Some female novelists find they are *still* more likely to be accepted for publication under a male pseudonym.[57]

Writing in schools

In school, writing serves a variety of purposes: it's a way for students to discover ideas; to explore their emotional responses to important questions and issues; to take their place in an academic conversation. And it's a mechanism to obtain qualifications, by conveying their knowledge in a clear and coherent way.

In some schools, an increased technical focus may have some benefits, but elsewhere it undermines the purpose of writing as exploratory, explanative and developmental. The Department for Education's teacher assessment framework for key stage 2 demands a mixture of accuracy and formality, but does contain some descriptions of genre and purpose. Writing at the expected standard, in a variety of topics and genres, students should be able to:

- Describe settings, characters and atmosphere.
- Integrate dialogue to advance the action.
- Describe and evaluate their own and others' scientific ideas.
- Write effectively for purposes and audiences, selecting language that shows good awareness of the reader.[58]

A GCSE English language mark scheme is, effectively, very similar. AQA's, for example, refers to "convincing communication" with accuracy and formality. Content criteria require that "tone, style and register are

---

57. Catherine Nichols, "Homme de plume: what I learned sending my novel out under a male name", *Jezebel*, 2015. Nichols sent out the same query as "Catherine" and as "George". George's manuscript was requested eight and a half times more than Catherine's

58. "Teacher assessment frameworks at the end of key stage 2", Department for Education, 2017

assuredly matched to purpose and audience" with "a range of convincing and compelling ideas".[59] In other subjects' exam papers, the purpose of writing is to explain ideas in detail, but guidance varies as to what the writing should actually be *like*.

Disciplinary literacy

Writing in some subjects can be incredibly formulaic. AQA's French exam, for example, gives a word count for most questions: 90 words to cover four bullet points. So, quite naturally in an exam-driven culture, students calculate that they need around 20 words per bullet point. The reduction of writing to a mere word count, even in a second language, diminishes the personal response that is essential. Elsewhere, writing accuracy is measured by a requirement to use appropriate subject terminology.

There is some movement to change this. AQA, for example, has recently suggested using the English teacher Becky Wood's "what, how, why" approach to English[60] as an open-ended scaffold, with far less reliance on subject terminology or overly complex vocabulary. Many teachers are ditching the acronyms in favour of a most academic exploration of what good writing is for a historian, geographer or biologist. A recent Education Endowment Foundation (EEF) guidance report on literacy suggests prioritising disciplinary literacy – "building on the premise that each subject has its own unique language, ways of knowing, doing, and communicating"[61] – that requires students to develop different styles of writing in each subject.

Other than exam-style answers, the dominant type of writing in secondary schools is the amorphous "creative writing". In the rest of the world, that phrase tends to mean fiction: novels, plays, short stories, poetry. In schools, it has come to mean anything that isn't a traditional

59. *English Language GCSE Specimen Mark Scheme*, AQA, 2015

60. Becky Wood, "Why I no longer PEE", *Just a Teacher Standing in Front of a Class* (blog), 28 October 2018, tinyurl.com/wkejsl8

61. Alex Quigley and Robbie Coleman, *Improving Literacy in Secondary Schools: guidance report*, Education Endowment Foundation, 5 July 2019

essay. In history, it might be a newspaper article or diary; in chemistry, it might be a leaflet; in religious studies, a poster.

As an English teacher, I'm all for writing in other subjects as much as possible, but this is a missed opportunity when it comes to disciplinary literacy. Other than exam success, disciplinary literacy is important for girls because it's a valuable real-world understanding of writing. Done well, it can build confidence, provide space for exploring that all-important identity and personal voice, and encourage girls to think about the kinds of writing they might encounter in different careers, thus opening up the careers conversation in a tangible way.

Real-world writing

Disciplinary literacy has to be real-world to have impact. If you're asking for a leaflet on the water cycle, for example, make it realistic. After all, these things are written about every day and giving students that clear understanding of task, audience and purpose helps them to think about how they explain their subject knowledge. If what you really want is an exam answer on the water cycle, ask them to write an exam answer. This has intrinsic value if you want students to know the details and how to express them in an exam. But it also offers the opportunity to broaden students' real-world experiences of the subject. Writing a double-page spread for a science book aimed at children aged 7–10 is a much more concrete brief. It has a specific audience, purpose and genre. It requires subject knowledge. It also echoes the kind of thing that scientists do all the time, which is make their knowledge accessible to a wide range of people.

Encourage students to take a few minutes to look at similar writing outputs and consider the language used, the presentation style and the choices the writer has had to make. Have they had to simplify their knowledge for their audience? Or use non-technical terms when there are technical ones available? Which is most appropriate for their task? Thinking about what you will leave *out* of your writing is often just as important as deciding what to put in. Girls and boys benefit when subjects are contextualised for them, and a huge part of most scientists' jobs (for example) is being able to effectively communicate with those who don't have their specialist knowledge. The act of writing for others also develops the wider culture of empathy and communication, pushing us to consider what they already know, what they need to know and how best to convey it.

A brief for writing an informational page

Genre	Biology book
Audience	Aged 7–10
Content	The water cycle. Double-page spread. 250 words
What they should know/think/feel after reading	• What the water cycle is • Some technical language • How people's actions change the water cycle
Explore the example double-page spread on biodiversity	
What features does the page use to make the information clear?	• Headline • Sidebar for technical language • Diagram in the middle with labels (1–3 words) • Bottom bar with an explanation • Short paragraphs with simple sentences • "Did you know?" balloon with unusual/interesting fact
How does the writer use specialist terms?	• In a sidebar; technical language is in bold and then explained in a simple way • No more than 10
How does the writer make the page interesting for their audience?	• Use of diagram and colour • Clear labels • Lots of space • Balloon for extra information
How does the writer show their specialist knowledge?	• Diagram is clear and cartoon-like, not complicated or like a photograph • Technical language that is all explained
Facts to include on the water cycle:	
Technical language to include:	

Three reasons to write

Firstly, writing is similar to oracy in that it's a way to explore thinking. In writing, though, there is greater need for clarity and precision. We're more willing to accept immediate revision and recasting when speaking because it's a less formal method of communication. In writing, we're forced to structure our thoughts differently. And when we do that, we often develop them into a more cohesive and connected understanding.

Secondly, writing is linked with academic success. In an exam, we must write clearly, precisely and at speed to be successful.

Thirdly, writing is good for our emotional and mental wellbeing.

One of the factors linking all these strands together is self-expression. Creative and academic writing both benefit from self-knowledge and self-awareness. Academic writing requires subject knowledge, but *really good* academic writing also needs you to understand, think about and evaluate what it is that you're writing – to be able to express your own opinions about it in your own voice.

Writing for discovery

Academic journaling is similarly useful for providing students with opportunities to consider their own ideas and responses, particularly in essay subjects. Allow five to 10 minutes at the beginning of the lesson for students to journal on a prompt (Is there such a thing as truth? How responsible is Juliet's nurse for the outcome of the play?) without worrying about subject vocabulary, phrasing or another reader. Journals are a means to get students thinking about their ideas and arguments. They are not intended to be read by others. They might provide the basis of a future discussion or essay, but they don't have to. They also give students confidence: I can write about my opinions, I *have* opinions!

We sometimes forget that the ending isn't always clear at the beginning, and that writing is a way to work through ideas. It's important that we reassure students that it's absolutely fine to end up somewhere other than where you thought you'd be, whether you're writing creatively or academically. In fact, this is to be encouraged and celebrated – it means that you're part of a conversation, a critical and compassionate thought process that listens to all perspectives and *then* comes to a decision. This more "feminine", collaborative and cooperative approach is sorely lacking in much public discourse, and so it's all the more necessary that we encourage it in the classroom.

It's useful to give students permission to say when they don't want us to read their work. Obviously, our professional judgement has to give us the confidence to say when they must hand work in, if they're trying to get out of doing it or if perfectionism has blinded them to its quality. When this happens, I have a conversation with students. Why isn't it right? What could work better? We usually manage to get the feedback they need – the feedback they can give themselves once they have undergone that process.

Conversations such as this normalise "failure" without calling it that. How devastating it can be to students when we tell them "it's OK to fail". The word itself is so loaded. I don't really believe that this is failure, in any case. The world is littered with half-novels and abandoned stories from writers who "failed" to finish them. It's a success to get halfway through an essay and realise that, actually, you think something else. Ideally, that happens before you get anywhere near an exam hall – the classroom is the perfect place for it.

Writing for academic success

Academic writing, particularly exam writing, is exceptionally complicated. The EEF's guidance report on literacy identifies three aspects of academic writing: composition (ideas, words, sentences), transcription (spelling and handwriting) and executive function (planning, motivation and reviewing).[62] Considering how to separate these three tasks through scaffolding can be a critical way to improve writing and build confidence.

To write well in exams, students have to be able to:

- Recall information.
- Synthesise it into an argument/answer.

---

62. Alex Quigley and Robbie Coleman, *Improving Literacy in Secondary Schools: guidance report,* Education Endowment Foundation, 5 July 2019

- Discard information that doesn't fit (even when it's accurate and they're desperate for an examiner to know that they know it!).
- Select appropriate vocabulary, especially tiers 2 and 3, and spell it correctly.
- Craft individual sentences for clarity and accuracy.
- Craft paragraphs that are clear, purposeful and fit together in the right order.
- Physically write for one or two hours at a time (which most students don't often do – it's rare in an hour-long lesson that they write at this speed for this length of time).
- Know how long they have to plan and write, and manage the time across the whole paper.
- Check (even mentally as they go) that they've included the right information for that subject, paper and question.
- Know the requirements of the subject, particularly command words like "describe" and "evaluate" (which are often different in different subjects).

That's a huge cognitive load, and all these processes have to coalesce in a short time period and under intense pressure. In the preparation stages, many girls in particular struggle with perfectionism when it comes to writing, especially those who want to please. They're scared of getting something wrong and being judged, and even if they know that a teacher is trying to support their improvement, they can struggle emotionally to accept feedback. Perfectionism can be crippling when it comes to writing, and although many girls overcome it in the exam, when the stakes are so high that they have little alternative, they've missed out on valuable practice.

Empathising with this struggle is important and so is separating the stages of writing. Debra Myhill's study of writing habits in Years 9–11 found that most students wrote in bursts, with pauses when they were planning, reassessing or editing. The highest-achieving students spent around two-thirds of their time writing and one-third pausing. These pauses were mostly used to forward-plan:

"When I pause, I'm not thinking about what I'm going to write next, I'm thinking about what's going to happen in two or three paragraphs' time."[63]

In contrast, lower achievers tend to use their pause time to plan the immediate next step, struggling with the cognitive load of planning. Most said they couldn't hold the plan in their head long enough to write it down.

Steps to reduce cognitive load

- **Use a repeated planning structure** (e.g. a graphical organiser or list) for each question, so that students can focus on what goes into the plan, not what form the plan should take. Routines are great for reducing cognitive load and building confidence.
- **Try temporary planning materials** such as whiteboards or Post-it notes. Something about these erasable, disposable methods helps students who struggle with perfectionism to unlock and get started.
- **Practise five-minute plans in lessons** so that students gain confidence. The bonus is that planning becomes a review-and-revise technique.
- **Backwards-plan essays.** From model answers, determine what the plan would have been, how much detail was needed, what kind of information was required, etc. Then students can forward-plan their own answer using the model.
- **Give feedback on planning** to reduce anxiousness about the content of ideas.
- **Try pair or group planning** for an individual essay.
- **Use structures that demonstrate a logical order**, e.g. if this, then that; or causes 1, 2 and 3, growing in severity. Connecting ideas makes them more memorable, as well as building a better essay!
- **Model how to go from plan to paragraph** so that the interim stage is clear. Too often we skip this section and assume it's a

---

63. Debra Myhill, "Children's patterns of composition and their reflections on their composing processes", *British Educational Research Journal*, 35:1, 2009

case of putting the plan into sentences, rather than explicitly modelling the shift from notes to writing academically.

- **Share a variety of sentence/essay openers**, modelling lots of techniques so students can choose a starting point from which to develop their independent voice.
- **Use repeated essay structures**, e.g. an introduction should include reference to the writer's message; a paragraph needs to include language analysis, reference to theme and context. Don't turn these into acronyms, which could become reductive. Use them more as mental checklists of what to include.
- **Try low-stakes quizzes to aid recall of critical information**, so that planning becomes about retrieving this information and then putting it in order.
- **Use academic journaling to determine an argument** before fleshing out the details with evidence.
- **Share frustration during modelling**. It's important to model the thought processes involved in writing, including frustration, thinking that the work isn't right or wanting to redraft it (but often not being able to due to time constraints).
- **Redraft with specific guidance/steps**, e.g. to replace tier 2 vocabulary with something more precise; to check for particular keywords.
- **Include a short "must-have" list** of essentials only. A short list is a good reminder; a long list only adds to cognitive anxiousness.
- **Use revision activities to reduce notes to the essentials**, in order to lessen cognitive load and focus on selection of materials.

Writing for emotional wellbeing

Writing is strongly connected to mental fitness: it plays a role in self-expression and self-understanding. Journaling is a good way to reduce the stress and anxiousness girls often experience. Techniques include:

- "Free writing" for 10 minutes without thought or prompt, to "empty your head". Simply writing down worries can make them seem less overwhelming. Free writing doesn't have to be based on problems, but can be whatever comes to mind.

- Writing based on a prompt, usually focusing on something positive.
- Writing a gratitude or thanks every day.

There are plenty of journals based on these principles. The most popular are "line a day" journals[64] – students are given a paper booklet with enough days for the academic year and every day they write something in it. The journal is not marked or even read by the tutor: it's a place for young people to reflect and find a moment of calm. Sometimes they write just a few words, sometimes they write a bit more and sometimes they fill an A5 page. It's up to them, but many of those who do it report feeling calmer and more centred as a result. Studies have suggested that writing about trauma enables a person to begin to process their experiences, while people with physical health conditions often find that expressive writing – once they get used to it – helps them to relax.[65] Similarly, students who write about their thoughts and feelings before an exam get better grades than those who don't.

That said, it's important to be mindful when using prompts designed to explore traumatic moments. Therapeutic writing can be upsetting and needs to be taken slowly, some time after the event. It's better to use prompts that are open-ended enough to allow students to explore trauma *if they wish*.

This kind of emotional writing often takes place in an inner world and an outer one:

- The "inner" world of our own experience of a situation – for example, in examining or metaphorising feelings of loss.
- The "outer" world of a situation of which we have first-hand knowledge.

---

64. A simple "line a day" journal PDF is available to download from my website, charlotteunsworth.com/resources

65. "Writing about emotions may ease stress and trauma", Harvard Health Publishing, accessed 2019

Writing about a health problem is both inner and outer. The inner experience is how we feel about it: how weak, tired, nauseous or afraid it might make us. The outer experience could be the relationships with others that form around it, or being pushed into poverty because of debilitating illness or isolation due to a broken leg.[66]

Writing in this way can build girls' emotional strength. Research into "bibliotherapy" suggests children's fears can be soothed through reading and writing, and that books provide opportunities to discuss, explore and overcome fears.[67] Writing is similar: prompts and reflection space can enable students to work through their ideas and concerns.

Addressing perfectionism

Whenever there's a chance of someone else reading a student's work, perfectionism can creep in (this doesn't just relate to writing and there are more strategies for this in chapter 14). Perfectionism can mean that the student can't even begin to write, or that they destroy their own work.

For those who have never experienced this feeling, let me tell you, it's horrendous. You want to write. You want to do what you've been asked to do: to do well and improve. You might even *know* that you really enjoy it, once you get started, but that blankness is a wall that seems impossible to climb. It can feel like your mind is empty of everything except the negative voice saying that you can't do this. It can genuinely feel like you can't move your hand to the page. It's crippling.

Perfectionism like this tends to affect girls more than boys, in part because of those early expectations of girls being good and right. Unfortunately, when it manifests in the ways I've described, it clashes with girls' expected behaviour of "getting on" and that creates further anxiousness. They want to please the person setting the task, but can't make their body and mind work in the way they want.

---

66. Fiona Sampson, "Writing as therapy", *The Handbook of Creative Writing*, ed. Steven Earnshaw, Edinburgh University Press, 2014

67. Janice I Nicholson and Quinn M Pearson, "Helping children cope with fears: using children's literature in classroom guidance", *Professional School Counseling*, 7:1, October 2003

I've found nothing as helpful as careful planning and redrafting, working to build resilience and reassuring students that you won't always read their work. After all, not every piece needs to be read and given feedback by teachers. If students can undertake structured self-assessment, using model answers as a benchmark, they might start to feel more confident that they can redraft and improve their work before handing it in.

- Do students have opportunities for reflective, emotional and exploratory writing across their subjects, and in PSHE or tutor time?
- Are distinctions made between these writing types in lessons, so students have clear outcomes for their work?
- Is writing always purposeful with a clear outcome?
- Is writing adequately scaffolded, with planning, sentence and paragraph structures developed and then gradually removed?
- Do students have checklists for self-assessment of work to reduce cognitive load?
- Do students have opportunities to write in structured and unstructured ways where they can experiment with their academic thought processes?
- Do subject teachers align their essay structures to reduce cognitive load for students?
- Are students given clear, repetitive planning structures for questions?
- Are students given instruction in different planning methods?
- Do teachers share their own writing struggles and empathise with students?
- Do teachers model writing in a way that shows their difficulties as well as their academic skill?

FURTHER RESOURCES

Julia Cameron's book **The Artist's Way** recommends "morning pages" or stream-of-consciousness writing first thing in the morning (or, for us, first lesson) to combat writer's block.

emagazine and other magazines also aimed at A-level students often accept submissions from students, giving them a real-life audience for their writing. *englishandmedia.co.uk/e-magazine*

Mslexia, a magazine for female writers, advertises writing workshops on its website and provides guidance on different styles. *mslexia.co.uk*

Judith C Hochman and Natalie Wexler's **The Writing Revolution** and Bridget Whelan's **Back to Creative Writing School** are excellent sources of inspiration for teaching extended writing.

4. Oracy

Speaking up and speaking out is the best way to claim equality. It might be speaking out about abuse to keep yourself safe, or advocating for a family member in an unfamiliar environment. It might be presenting in a workplace, interviewing for a job or asking for a pay rise. It might be participating in a conversation about politics, education or what you think is the right thing to do in a certain situation. It might be saying, "That makes me uncomfortable" or "I think that's a great decision". Women need the confidence to speak out in all aspects of their lives.

There are two main reasons to develop female students' oracy. The first is to empower them to speak up for themselves and others, to share their ideas openly and be heard. The second is to shift the way that oracy is perceived, away from its classical origins rooted in patriarchal performance and show. The aim is for all students, no matter their understanding of rhetoric, to be heard and to listen in a way that is empathetic and genuinely communicative – a dialogue rather than a one-sided speech.

Studies show that women in business and politics are repeatedly silenced in different ways.[68] They're given less speaking time, interrupted more (and more negatively by men)[69] and asked more complex "gate-keeping" questions. Here are some common scenarios in meetings and conferences:

- Mid-discussion, a woman offers an idea to the group. She's interrupted by a man who says almost exactly the same thing. His comments are accepted and praised.
- In a Q&A, a male audience member puts up his hand and offers a lengthy critique of a female panel member's work, without asking a question.
- A woman starts to speak but is interrupted by someone. She waits until they've finished, but is then interrupted by someone else.

In schools, the term oracy is associated more with classroom discussion and presentations than the closed questioning of recall and swift revision, although this is often a good way to build confidence. An oracy focus benefits all pupils, particularly those disadvantaged young people who, according to the National Literacy Trust, contribute just four words per lesson (and those are likely to be procedural rather than related to their learning).

---

68. Judith Baxter, *Double-Voicing at Work: power, gender and linguistic expertise,* Palgrave Macmillan, 2014

69. Adrienne B Hancock and Benjamin A Rubin, "Influence of communication partner's gender on language", *Journal of Language and Social Psychology,* 34:1, January 2015

A culture of silencing

Good public speaking is associated with charisma and confidence, and we're more likely to believe that confident people are capable (even without further proof). There is, though, a surprisingly fine line between confident delivery and confidence in the subject matter and an arrogant, blustering show with little substance.

In her book *Women and Power*, the historian Mary Beard traces the patriarchal power of public speech back to the Greek and Roman traditions of oracy. She starts with the silencing of Penelope in Homer's *The Odyssey* and continues to the lack of female space in political arenas. She argues that an "integral part of growing up, as a man, is learning to take control of public utterance and to silence the female of the species".[70] In the classical world, women can speak only as victims or in defence of their own interests: their families, their husbands and other women. She cites this eerily familiar line from a second-century commentator:

> *"A woman should as modestly guard against exposing her voice to outsiders as she would guard against stripping off her clothes."*

Beard is no stranger to suggestions that she should sit down and shut up, or that a woman's power is inherently associated with her looks. She experiences frequent online abuse for her opinions, while commentary on her television work is as likely to discuss her appearance as it is her ideas (if not more likely). And it's not just what women say that brings censure, but also how they say it. The very sound and pitch of women's voices are often criticised as "shrill" or "croaky". Vocal fry, a slightly creaky vocal mannerism, has been associated with weakness and women who use this speech pattern thought of as less trustworthy and less educated.[71] The feminist linguist Deborah Cameron argues against this:

---

70. Mary Beard, *Women and Power: a manifesto*, Profile Books, 2017
71. Naomi Wolf, "Young women, give up the vocal fry and reclaim your strong female voice", *The Guardian*, 24 July 2015

"This endless policing of women's language – their voices, their intonation patterns, the words they use, their syntax – is uncomfortably similar to the way our culture polices women's bodily appearance."[72]

It's too common for girls and women to be taught to change how they speak, right down to pitch and tone – to aim for "more authoritative" speech. Margaret Thatcher is just one example of a woman who underwent vocal coaching and was told to lower her voice, using a deeper register and less variation. Recent studies suggest that a politician's lower, more masculine pitch still significantly influences voting behaviours.[73] This reinforces the idea that women simply don't have authority *because they are women*. When we teach rhetoric, debating or public speaking, we often teach classical masculine structures and devices. Shouldn't we instead be teaching girls that their voices have power because they have something to say and a right to be heard?

Like so much of this, it's a difficult balance. Where does teaching girls to speak up for themselves end and teaching them to become more "masculine" to be successful begin? Do rhetorical techniques create an air of confidence *because* they are associated with powerful male speech? Disadvantaged pupils are subject to the same silencing that Beard sees happening to women. Teaching oracy as part of their cultural capital is one way to help them overcome the barriers before them, but it doesn't do the far harder task of breaking those barriers down and encouraging people to talk on their own terms. There needs to be a balance of both.

Politically and socially we're at an interesting time, in which public discourse might be on the brink of being redefined. Wouldn't it be refreshing to have authentic, honest voices in our public arenas? Voices

72. Deborah Cameron, "Just don't do it", *Language: A Feminist Guide* (blog), 5 July 2015, tinyurl.com/naz98zb

73. Cara C Tigue, Diana J Borak, Jillian JM O'Connor, Charles Schandl and David R Feinberg, "Voice pitch influences voting behaviour", *Evolution and Human Behavior*, 33:3, May 2012

that are reflective, thoughtful and engaged with issues on a personal level, rather than indulging in ancient rhetoric and elusive metaphor? What if public speaking became more of a conversation, where presenters genuinely engaged with listeners in order to extend thinking on a subject until consensus was reached?

Oracy supports the written demonstration of learning, too. By being able to articulately express themselves orally, students are better prepared to write, whether it's short-answer questions or an essay. Elsewhere, improved oracy is associated with better emotional and mental wellbeing.[74] Children need to be able to express themselves in order to be safe and feel listened to. Mentally healthy schools hold open discussions not just about mental fitness, but about a wide range of issues that might be on children's minds. Rather than ruminating or worrying, young people can speak about their concerns.

Barriers to classroom oracy

Education studies show that girls' oracy begins to suffer in the classroom. Debra Myhill's study of classroom interaction found that underachievers were less likely to contribute to discussion and high-achieving boys were dominant.[75] Across primary classrooms, Myhill writes, "boys call out considerably more than girls although the underachieving boys are more likely to call out than their high-achieving peers". Other studies agree that boys dominate the classroom.[76]

As teachers, we forget how difficult it is to speak in front of 30 other people (until we lead a whole-school CPD session!). Students may fear their voice failing; being wrong and looking stupid; being right and looking like a geek. These fears can become self-perpetuating. There's also a kind of frustration for many girls: the "me, again?" feeling of always being asked to explain things to others.

---

74. *Speaking Frankly: the case for oracy in the curriculum*, English-Speaking Union, 2016

75. Debra Myhill, "Bad boys and good girls? Patterns of interaction and response in whole class teaching", *British Educational Research Journal*, 28:3, 2002

76. M Warrington, M Younger and J Williams, "Student attitudes, image and the gender gap", *British Educational Research Journal*, 26:3, 2000

We know there is value in debate and discussion; in being pushed to develop and evaluate your own ideas as well as exploring someone else's. Let's make this explicit to students: we are not only looking for their ideas or some "guess what's in my head" answer. We are looking for a debate that considers a range of perspectives and works to find common ground. Agreement might sometimes be reached, but in many cases it won't. We can agree to disagree – a fundamental part of conversation and dialogue – in a way that is respectful of others' opinions and genuinely considers what they have to say.

Classroom conversations

Everyone – girls and boys – benefits when whole-class discussion is academic, thoughtful and collaborative, rather than an opportunity to express an individual perspective without follow-up. Again, there is some value in the quick answer-response to check basic understanding, but that oracy serves a very different purpose for us as teachers.

We can help students in class discussion by using no-hands-up questioning and ensuring that there is an expectation that students speak regularly throughout the school day. The longer students are permitted to remain silent through choice, as students who experience anxiousness often will, the worse that anxiousness will become, until speaking may well be impossible. Selective mutism affects more girls than boys and around one in 140 children. It's a more extreme version of social anxiety, where children may be able to speak freely in some situations (with parents or friends) but feel unable to do so in others (with teachers, for example). Like many anxieties, selective mutism starts small and progresses, often requiring specialist intervention at a later stage. Clearly, we have to be aware of the needs of students in our care. But if we allow a teaching practice to develop where students are able to stay silent all day, then we permit the possibility of such anxiousness worsening.

Here is some practical and simple guidance for class discussion:

- Make it as low-stakes as possible so students are willing to respond.
- Allow thinking time so everyone has the opportunity to decide what to say. If necessary, students can first write some notes on responses.

- Set clear listening expectations.
- Comments should respond to what has gone before.
- Give clear instructions on how to ask others to speak up – sometimes this is necessary, particularly if someone in the room above decides it's the moment for all the students to push their chairs back at once! Having a conversation about the right, polite way to do it can be helpful.
- Discuss how to clarify answers and model the same. We should explicitly talk about how to ask someone in a supportive way to explain their meaning or recast what they have said.
- Use sentence starters or frameworks, just like in writing.
- Scaffold discussion from pair to group to whole class.
- Monitor who speaks and who doesn't, to ensure all students have the chance to speak regularly.

Starters for speech

Agreeing	Clarifying
• I agree with X because… • X's point about Y was important because… • Although I'm not sure about everything X was saying, I think that they're right about…	• So is what you're saying that… • Is it right that you're saying… • I'm confused about Y, could you explain?
Developing	**Challenging**
• X mentioned that… • Yes, and also… • That's an interesting idea, because later… • Adding to what X said… • If you look at it from this point instead…	• I see it differently because… • I think this shows something else to think about Y… • I agree with X but when you look at Y… • I don't think the same about Y because…

We can also be more explicit about the role of developmental talk and recasting in an academic register. This encourages high achievers to participate and see class discussion as a useful way to explore and plan for their own work, rather than a way for teachers to test understanding, which is when they're more likely to check out. Using Cornell notes or whiteboard mind-mapping to capture discussions is a good way to demonstrate the skills required to synthesise ideas. With practice, an able class can pass this "minute-taker" responsibility around, demonstrating the importance of high-quality talk that contributes to deeper understanding.

Public speaking

There is a distinct difference between class discussion (sitting safely in your seat, a sentence or two, more casual language) and presentations (everyone focused on you, standing at the front, often alone, higher expectations). Teachers can see off many potential difficulties by openly discussing the fact that a difference exists and exploring the demands of these two formats in the same way we would written registers. The concept of a shared experience is supportive enough for many to feel empowered.

There should be lots of opportunities for practice, as familiarity alone will help to boost the confidence of many students. Broken down, the components of public speaking include:

- Having a speech of a certain length in a "good" style (one that engages with the audience, conveys the ideas you want in the time available, and uses language that is clear and interesting).
- Being able to stand and gesture in a way that adds to the performance.
- Being able to move your gaze from the page to the audience confidently, making eye contact as you would in a conversation.
- Being able to speak at a volume, pitch and pace that connects with the audience and makes you feel comfortable.

Good practice begins in classroom discussion

The work of the psychologist Amy Cuddy and others reinforces the idea that body language matters, helping to engage the listener and make the speaker feel more confident.[77] An "expansive" (Wonder Woman) posture

---

77. Amy JC Cuddy, S Jack Schultz and Nathan E Fosse, "P-curving a more comprehensive body of research on postural feedback reveals clear evidential value for power-posing effects: reply to Simmons and Simonsohn", *Psychological Science*, 29:4, 2018

held for two minutes created feelings of power and confidence: subjects performed better in mock interviews. Subjects who held "low power poses" (leaning inwards, arms and legs crossed) performed less well. An expansive pose takes up space: the body communicates to the mind, "You matter. You can have space here, it's OK." A low-power pose says, "Hide. You don't belong."

As with most skills, this can be developed. In the classroom, encourage students to sit up straight, arms comfortable and loose on the desk. When it comes to presentation, deliberately teach gesture as a way to avoid fidgeting that could be distracting or suggest nervousness. The former US president Barack Obama is a good example: his hand gestures changed significantly between his nomination and the middle of his first presidency. Over time, they became more expansive, confident and deliberate. Acknowledge that gesturing might *feel* awkward at first, but it *looks* natural and helps to emphasise key points. Get students to think about the way they move their hands in normal conversation and how they can make their presentations feel more comfortable.

Readjusting posture is the same as recasting words in an academic register. Explicitly teaching this, by comparing poses, is a good way to get students thinking about it. When students deliver short presentations of a minute or so, pause them a few seconds in, adjust their posture and ask them to continue (obviously, judge your students' resilience here).

Using notes well

The right notes can be a huge confidence boost. Public speakers might not always use notes, but the vast majority will have either notes or a teleprompter, and it's perfectly acceptable for students to emulate this.

Even modelling a good way to prepare notes can build confidence. When speaking, I use a large 18-point sans-serif font on A5 paper, single-sided and double-spaced. I show these notes to students. I also mark them up: because I studied music at school, I use notation to remind me to breathe, slow down, change volume and pause. Some students find this too much and would prefer something like capitalised sub-headings to help them concentrate on individual sections or insert strategic pauses.

Regular practice

If the only presentations students do with deliberate practice are their languages speeches and their GCSE English presentations, then it's not much of a surprise when they find them inordinately stressful. We have to provide frequent opportunities for public speaking and explicitly teach the skills we value.

Adopt a whole-school standard for presentations. I like the "five a slide" rule, where students can use images or up to five words for a PowerPoint slide – or no slides at all. If every teacher uses this rule, the expectations are clear, minimising the cognitive load again and creating a safety net of sorts.

Every subject teacher can incorporate presentations into their lessons. If they aren't a formal assessment, we can still comment on the presentation quality as well as the content. If they are a formal assessment, then presentation quality should be assessed just as you would spelling, punctuation and grammatical clarity in a written text.

Extracurricular opportunities matter, too. Debating can have stringent structures that can be adapted for beginners or learned for the purposes of inter-school competitions, but it can be a tricky method of developing girls' oracy. It's traditionally exceptionally masculine, and common in spheres of power like high-status public schools, parliaments and courts. It has strict rules and a vocabulary all its own, and can be intimidating for anyone unused to the particular brand of confidence it often seems to bestow. But the structures of debating can be learned. Students don't have to perform aggressively: they can debate, discuss and argue persuasively without being overpowering or overbearing, and they can win competitions against those who think they have it made. Many university debating teams run outreach programmes with schools and can provide support in training students. Plenty also run school competitions (including Durham, Cambridge, Manchester and Oxford) and offer weekend events and training; for many of my GCSE students, this is the first time they experience a university. Internal events like TedX or Project Soapbox can be great ways of encouraging short speeches to build confidence.

Assemblies can also be led and presented by students. At my school, students select topics from a list at the beginning of the year, then write and prepare in their tutor groups. They deliver the assembly four times in a week to each house group. Presenting as a group scaffolds the experience: each individual stands, but speaks only a little. Students are also asked to present to one another: sixth-formers advise Year 11 on revision techniques, for example, or speak to incoming students, parents and governors. Remember the good girls: do we always ask the same students because we know they'll deliver? Or do we neglect to ask some girls because they seem very quiet? Everyone should have the opportunities to do these kinds of public presentations.

Students could also be encouraged to present on something on which they are an expert. Nothing builds confidence like sharing something you love, so an opportunity for a student to discuss "their thing" can be incredibly valuable. My school has held sessions where students teach skills like knitting or origami to others. Focusing on a physical task, rather than on the people watching them, enabled them to talk with confidence and self-assurance, particularly in smaller groups.

Presentation standards

①   Convey your ideas

- Decide your key message before you start. What do you want your audience to think, feel or know that they didn't before you spoke to them?
- Make this clear at the beginning and the end.
- Go for balance – you could use an academic register to convey your ideas because this is a more formal situation, but keep a sense of your own voice so the audience can connect with you.

②   Think flow

- Use PowerPoint tools to embed video and audio, rather than swapping software.
- How will people move to and from the microphone?
- Where can you slow down for "pause points" to enable reflection?
- What is your ending? Make it clear so an audience knows that this is their time to reflect on what you have said.

Visuals

- PowerPoint slides should have limited words – fewer than 20 – and include headings or images as visual cues for an audience.
- Slides should not be your script – you should be adding content in your speech.
- Text needs to be legible from the back of the room, so think about size and colour. In the hall, it shouldn't be less than 28pt to be readable.

Prepare

- Use notecards or cue cards.
- Give everyone their own copy of the script.
- Know your topic and your script – you should read it aloud several times before speaking in public.
- Although you don't have to learn it by heart, it should be familiar enough that you can look up and connect with your audience.

Stand confidently

- Stand tall.
- Stand squarely.
- In gatherings, use standing microphones or the lectern.
- Avoid fidgeting.
- Decide what to do with your hands – do you gesture when you talk? Or would you rather your hands held something like the script or the lectern?
- What will you be doing when someone else is speaking?

Keep it slow

- We speak faster than we think.
- Conversation is roughly 150–180 words per minute (wpm). A good speech to an audience is around 120 wpm, so try to slow down.
- Use paragraph breaks to mark pauses on your script.
- It can help to make some words bold – for example, the beginning of a point – so you can see them at a glance.
- A six-minute speech at 120 wpm is roughly one side of A4 in 11pt text.
- Try to pause instead of using filler words such as "like" or "um".

Vocabulary

It's completely acceptable to challenge students to speak in an academic way that is grammatically accurate, with appropriately formal structures. It's important to discuss the difference between dialect (speech associated with a region), idiolect (speech associated with an individual's identity, often combining slang from different influences) and a formal register.

We should celebrate students' idiolects. Use of our own personal language can convey authenticity, as well as making us feel more comfortable. Being able to drop into idiolect can cement a relationship, create an impression of who we are, or make a significant point. But it's not appropriate at all times. We owe it to all our students to make sure they know what the right time is and how to speak when it's not.

We can model this ourselves, too, making it explicit to students that we might speak in different registers in different situations – even in the classroom compared with the corridor, or with Year 7 compared with Year 13. By speaking in the elaborated code, using the academic register, we can constantly model language to students.

What next steps can I take?

- In the classroom, consider gender bias in questioning.
- Use tactics to promote turn-taking and discussion (even a talking stick if students find it hard!). Ensure that the questions being posed to girls and boys are equally challenging.
- Allow students time to consider their responses. Research shows that everyone benefits from the opportunity to think about what someone is saying before a response is required.
- Gently challenge interruptions by directing back to the original speaker. The interrupter can still have their say – it's a conversation, after all – but their contribution should acknowledge the previous comments.
- Explicitly teach body postures and hand gestures as part of presentations.
- Consider introducing a whole-school presentation standard with basic guidelines for all students and staff.

- Do subjects offer regular chances for students to practise oracy, in both class discussion and formal presentations?
- Are there opportunities to offer oral assessments, e.g. presentations or viva-style discussions?
- Do the rhetorical structures and presentational styles expected of students come from a masculine authority, or do they seek to grant students authority through their experiences?
- Are girls and boys asked roughly equal questions (in terms of number and content) in the classroom?
- Are classroom discussions managed respectfully, with all students able to contribute?
- Do students respond to one another in class discussion, or does all conversation filter through the teacher?
- Do teachers regularly use no-hands-up questioning to ensure that boys and girls are involved in the conversation?
- Are students given time to think, reflect and plan so they are confident in what they can say?
- Are the presentational skills of body language, note-making and audience engagement taught alongside content creation?
- Do teachers have a clear view of what is required in presentations?
- Is there a school-wide presentation standard?

FURTHER RESOURCES

Debating Matters offers information on debating structures and preparation. *debatingmatters.com*

The English Speaking Union debating organisation promotes speaking and listening skills in schools, and offers CPD. *esu.org*

Speaking Frankly, a report by the English Speaking Union on the value of oracy, contains suggestions for classroom activities. *tinyurl.com/uzscxwm*

The Noisy Classroom is a PiXL group that supports speaking and listening in the classroom. The website lists national debating/speaking competitions. *noisyclassroom.com/secondary-oracy-activities*

Toastmasters runs public-speaking clubs that can often help in finding coaches or judges. *toastmasterclub.org*

Youth Speaks is a public-speaking competition run by Rotary International. The organisation can often provide contacts for coaches or judges for intra-school contests. *rotarygbi.org/projects/young-people/competitions*

5. English

Representation of the world, like the world itself,
is the work of men; they describe it from their
own point of view, which they confuse with
absolute truth – Simone de Beauvoir, *The Second Sex*

I would venture to guess that Anon, who wrote
so many poems without signing them, was often
a woman – Virginia Woolf, *A Room of One's Own*

English teachers have a unique opportunity because the subject offers such incredible flexibility of curriculum, even at GCSE. The possibility of adding breadth in the unseen extracts and poetry means we can explore writers of any time period, gender, age, ethnicity, sexuality and country of origin.

The canon

At GCSE, most exam boards adopt a broadly new historicist approach to literary study, in which students are expected to consider the social, historical and literary contexts of the writer. Many of the named writers are white men and the text choice is broadly canonical, which has its pros and cons. Discussing this with students encourages them to see the canon as a list from a particular time and place in society that is open to adaptation and change. Contemporary reviews can be a great way to challenge the canon – reviews of *Jane Eyre* at the time of publication, for example, were often quite negative and provide a way to discuss the difficulties of "predicting" what becomes a "classic" novel.

If we want students to have access to the best that has been thought and said, we have to open the curriculum up to the best *in all cultures*. Students can also participate in the discussion of what culture is and could be. As the teacher and blogger Jennifer Webb has said, culture is two things: firstly, the heritage, arts and self-expression of an individual; secondly, what someone in power has deemed worthy of study.[78] We have the right and responsibility, as do our students, to question where that power comes from and whether it remains valid. Arguably, the mark of a truly great book, poem or play is whether it enters one's soul and becomes part of one's self-expression. It's our job as teachers to give students as broad a perspective as possible, to enable them to make informed and knowledgeable decisions about what speaks to them as individuals and what is "good quality". Both are subjective.

As teachers, we can also challenge the exam boards to diversify their canon.[79] Here's what is currently on offer from the exam boards for English literature in terms of gender balance:

Exam board	19th-century text choices	Modern text choices	Poetry collections
AQA	3 female, 4 male	2 female, 9 male	4 or 5 female out of 15
Edexcel	4 female, 3 male	5 female, 7 male	6 or 7 female out of 15
Eduqas	3 female, 4 male	4 female, 6 male	5 female out of 15
OCR	2 female, 4 male	2 female, 4 male	6 or 7 female out of 15

78. Jennifer Webb, "Storming the Citadel: a quest for cultural capital", *FunkyPedagogy* (blog), 25 June 2019, tinyurl.com/sdy233s

79. Arguably, this is very difficult – part of the canonical quality is surely longevity and continued relevance. But some success is possible

These choices are hardly what you would call diverse – although, given that two works by Dickens appear on most board lists, the 19th-century choices actually offer a wider variety of female authors than male, unlike the modern choices. Even Edexcel's decision to add "diverse" options doesn't help hugely when it comes to *positive* representation, particularly of ethnic minorities, in the modern text selection.

A wider view

English is interesting in a whole-school curriculum because of the sheer breadth of ideas that teachers will try to cover. The 2019 AQA examiner's report included this comment towards the end, about the persuasive writing question:

> *"What characterised the best of these responses was the ability to engage with the 'big ideas': politics, economics, gender, aesthetics, class, morality, psychology, even philosophy. Students who were confident and familiar with these ideas were able to frame their own perspectives in this larger context and thereby enhance the quality of their argument."*[80]

That's a massive ask for any student, never mind demonstrating this kind of renaissance thinking in just 45 minutes. And yet, English teachers strive to enable their students to meet the challenge. On Twitter, resources covering an astounding variety of issues are being shared:

- "Resources for Paper 2 – texts cover technology, poverty, mental health, careers, violence, sexism, drugs."
- "Created scheme on news about banning smacking."
- " ... themes such as riots, child poverty, packed lunches...!"
- "Mock papers: employment law, democracy and poverty."

---

80. *GCSE English Language 8700/2: Paper 2 – report on the examination,* AQA, 2019

Opening up these broad conversations is one of the most exhilarating aspects of English teaching. It's absolutely necessary for girls to be able to explore, challenge and be challenged by these ideas. Just as we saw in the chapters on biology and socialisation, there are big assumptions out there that go unquestioned, and many of those will have a direct impact on the girls in our classroom.

English is also the ideal place to explore female voices on topics that are not simply, as Mary Beard suggests, restricted to "women's interests". We can look at women's political writing, their personal letters, speeches and much more, on as wide a variety of topics as possible.

Intersectional feminism

Intersectional feminism explores how all aspects of social and political identities overlap – class, ethnic background, sexuality, ability, country of origin, age and gender. When we audit our curriculum for gender diversity, let's look at a broader range. Are we expecting Meera Syal and Malorie Blackman to be representative of all non-white female experiences? Or have we made deliberate efforts to ensure that there are genuine representations from a wide range of backgrounds?

Challenging traditional representation is really important, as Gretchen Gerzina explores in her work on Victorian-era African American writers. She points out that we often assume black writers had limited literacy and wrote solely about experiences of slavery and struggle:

> "Because we didn't realise that authors like [Sarah E] Farro existed, we had limited our perspective on their work ... As [the literary scholar Elizabeth] McHenry writes, 'the danger of privileging [slave narratives] is that we risk overlooking the many other forms of literary production that coexisted alongside [them]."[81]

---

81. Gretchen Gerzina, "After the rediscovery of a 19th-century novel, our view of black female writers is transformed", *The Conversation*, 26 May 2016

This holds true, too, for other marginalised groups. There is a lot more women's writing than we think, but sometimes we have to search a little harder for it.

When we're considering the diversity of the curriculum, let's look at what we're reading women's writing on. Black women shouldn't be restricted to writing about "black women's issues", or women with Indian heritage to writing about colonialist India. Writers have the right to write about what they find interesting and important. Our responsibility as teachers is to look at their work and ask: is this a good, fair and accurate representation? Does it teach us something, or ask us to question something?

Female writers, female characters

To value women's role in society and the traditionally feminine qualities, we have to consider the way that women are represented as both writers and characters. When we select literary texts, we can choose to incorporate female writers in all aspects of our teaching practice, and we can choose to balance the curriculum. And when we teach texts, we can explore gender representation and balance.

When I teach *Jekyll and Hyde*, for example, it not only brings some gender balance but makes sense to discuss Mary Shelley's *Frankenstein* from 70 years earlier, and compare the representations of science and monstrosity.

Sample lesson ideas

Lesson		
Key questions	• What are the similarities and differences between Jekyll and Frankenstein? (Lit, AO1, AO3) • Why do the writers use this confessional style? (Lit, AO2) • How is science viewed by writers at different points of the 19th century? (Lang, AO2, AO4)	**Resources** Frankenstein chapter 4: "No one can conceive…my work near to a conclusion"
Exploratory writing	Who can you think of that would be called a "mad scientist" and what caused their experiments to go horribly wrong? *May discuss ideas e.g. working alone, megalomania, desire to do good becomes distorted*	

Learning activities/ opportunities for writing and self-expression	• Read and discuss *Frankenstein* (Paper 1 language practice). • Search for similarities to Jekyll's "statement of the case", e.g. references to being a father, attitude to science, motifs/ imagery, the characters' feelings of powerlessness, addiction (to power itself?), Gothic imagery. • Explore how the writers both use first-person, confessional narratives for this section of the story. What is the impact of this? • Discuss the feeling of power given to the characters through the exploration of science. How does this connect with exploratory-writing ideas from the start? What is the social fear behind the "mad scientist" trope?

Although it would be made clear that Mary Shelley was female in the introduction to *Frankenstein*, it wouldn't necessarily be explicit in class discussion. But it could be, for example, when discussing the likely influence *Frankenstein* had on *Jekyll and Hyde*.

When teaching *Jekyll and Hyde*, I usually explore the presentation of masculinity and discuss why the novel is entirely lacking in women. I consider the redirection of the female gaze towards Hyde (it is the women who do the watching) as a potential indicator of repressed homosexuality being Jekyll's mysterious "pleasures".

Lesson		
Key questions	• Who are the women in the novel? What are their roles/actions? (Lit, AO1) • How is the idea of the male gaze subverted in this novel? (Lit, AO3) • How do men and women represent the city in different forms? (Lit, AO2)	**Resources** Extracts of critical opinions, e.g. Marianne Manzler on new women, quotes by Shelby Lueders, Laura Mulvey, Janice Doane, Greg Buzwell
Exploratory writing	Why do you think there are no women in major roles in the novel?	
Learning activities/ opportunities for writing and self-expression	• Using Charles Campbell quotation on representation of the city, list times/places where women are seen in the novel. • Read/discuss further critical commentaries, using supporting questions to probe ideas, e.g. who are the women associated with? What are their roles? Who watches who and when? Do the women play a moral role? • Read critical information on homosexuality and blackmail (Greg Buzwell). Discuss application to *Jekyll and Hyde*. • Practice-writing paragraph: what is one interpretation of the origins of Hyde?	

When we're teaching fiction texts, it can be useful to include either non-fiction (letters in particular), criticism or fiction that explores the way women were perceived at the time. The British Library is absolutely amazing when it comes to GCSE texts especially – its range of critical work is brilliant and it often has original sources that can offer some fascinating challenge for students. For *Romeo and Juliet*, for example, the library has William Gouge's *Of Domesticall Duties* (1622), which explains the best age for someone of Shakespeare's era to be married and challenges many students' perception that everyone got married at Juliet's age.

English teachers aren't history teachers. But we see the past through the lens of the texts we use, and it's important that we challenge the simplistic idea that "women in history were rubbish", which itself perpetuates harmful gender stereotypes. By characterising women in history as domestic, victims of men, powerless, weak, vulnerable and so on, we create a long line of victimhood that only confirms women's weaker position. In reality, we know that this is not the universal history of women across the world. "Power" means different things at different times to different people. Giving the impression that women were helplessly enslaved for centuries doesn't empower our current generation of young women, and it also does a disservice to those women who did struggle against patriarchal restraint.

Equally, we want young women and men to see that women in society have, mainly because of their biological reproductive status, often been kept from the opportunities and social experiences that have enabled men over generations to hold the power and wealth that currently give them their privileged place in society.

Teenagers need to recognise this historical sexism because it directly contributes to current sexist attitudes. But it doesn't mean that we're condemned to repeat the past, and teaching the complexities of women's status in history, as seen in literature, can help us to explore the nuances of equality today and engage in dialogue about the shades of grey in our black and white view of gender.

The questions we ask about texts are important. It is necessary to ask "How are women represented in X" or "How far is X represented as an independent woman", not least because this is a common style of GCSE essay question. For many students, the term "women in history" conjures up a universally horrendous and remarkably homogeneous female existence in the dim and distant past (before about 1980 at the moment, it seems). We need to challenge this.

Frequently, the lack of nuance reveals itself in blanket contextual bolt-ons like "Lady Macbeth is shocking because she's powerful, and not controlled by her husband". This is often supported with statements that women were inferior and less powerful, or some vague surprise that Lady Macbeth wasn't more busy cleaning her (surely dusty and very muddy) castle. We can dispute this on several counts:[82]

- Lady Macbeth is wealthy and high-status – she becomes queen. She would not have been cooking, cleaning or "domestic" in the way that is often suggested.
- She's not the only powerful woman in Shakespeare's plays. By the time of writing *Macbeth*, he had already created Juliet, Portia, Beatrice, Viola and Desdemona. Audiences expected strong and challenging women from him.
- Audiences were used to powerful women. Many would have lived through Elizabeth I's reign, and some Mary I's too. Given that Elizabeth had come to the throne 48 years before the first performance of *Macbeth*, it's entirely likely that most of their lives had been lived under a queen rather than a king.
- At the time, women were publicly known and discussed, including Mary Queen of Scots, Bess of Hardwick and Margaret Pole. They weren't hidden away.

With characters like Lady Macbeth, we can also discuss their representation and how it reflects a tradition of trying to control women's "natural" violent, evil and transgressive urges (no evolutionary biology in Shakespeare's time!). Her sexuality is critical: much of her language links sex and gender inextricably together, and the repeated references to

---

82. The Twitter account @GCSE_Macbeth has hosted discussions on this topic with some superb detail

infertility make her something quite dangerous in biological terms. She doesn't appear to be someone for whom childbirth and rearing is going to take priority, and therefore she has the ability to enter traditionally male spaces without restriction.

We can explore Lady Macbeth's connection with witches and the way that the word "witch" is typically used as a way to label, accuse and punish women. Non-fiction texts or other extracts are excellent for context here: the journalist Rhiannon Lucy Cosslett explores witches from a feminist perspective,[83] Laura Bates's novel *The Burning* places modern attitudes towards sexting and female sexuality alongside the Scottish "witch" trials of the 1600s,[84] and choices like Arthur Miller's play *The Crucible* create an often missing opportunity to incorporate some drama into the curriculum. An excellent essay by Sandra M Gilbert[85] explores how Lady Macbeth goes beyond prescribed gender roles and includes insightful comments from actors who have portrayed her. With these short comments, students can engage not only with interpretations of the character, but also with how these interpretations are affected by the gendered roles of the times in which the actors lived.

Shakespeare also offers lovely opportunities to explore the concept of gender as performative. What better play than, say, *Twelfth Night*, where a male actor plays a female character playing a male version of herself?

Compassion and empathy

English helps girls and boys to feel confident in expressing their thoughts and opinions, valuing the role of empathy and communication for everybody. Students need help to express, shape and deliver these thoughts. One brilliant tool for expanding emotional vocabulary is the emotions wheel. Ask students to choose a hierarchy of words to describe a character at a given moment and invite them to contrast emotions across a text.

83. Rhiannon Lucy Cosslett, "From Baba Yaga to Hermione Granger: why we're spellbound by 'witcherature'", *The Guardian*, 12 August 2019

84. Laura Bates, *The Burning*, Simon & Schuster, 2019

85. Sandra M Gilbert, "'Unsex me here': Lady Macbeth's 'hell broth'", British Library, 15 March 2016

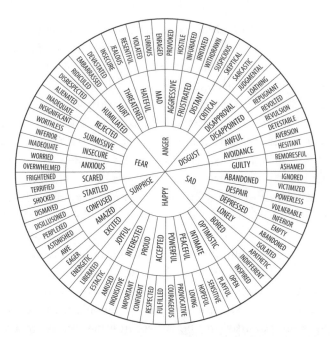

When it comes to developing empathy, character analysis is a gift. Asking students to explicitly explore motivations and feelings demands that they "slip inside the skin of another"[86] and develop their compassion. Try these questions to help them do this:

- Why is she like this?
- What is prompting her to act in this way?
- What do you think she would be thinking now?
- What do you think she will feel about this later?
- What do you think she will do about this feeling later?
- What would you do in her place?
- What would be an alternative response to this?
- How would that change things?
- Why do you think she's in this position?
- What would you advise her to do?

86. Lloyd Jones, *Mister Pip*, John Murray, 2006

From these questions, we can start to discuss our own opinions about situations, modelling a more compassionate approach to others. Talking with empathy builds students' ability to consider the treatment of marginalised groups or those labelled as "other". As English teachers, we do much of this kind of questioning almost without thinking, and it can get lost in "plot development" discussions before we get on to the "real work" of analysing language, but it's fundamental to the study of literature and crucial to the development of empathy.

We can also ask students to identify which emotions might typically be associated with which gender, and to explore how far those stereotypes hold true in the texts they read. Girls often express more sadness than boys, but are taught to repress their anger. Meanwhile, boys are taught to repress their sadness. Internalising and externalising emotions can both be damaging in the wrong context.[87] These stereotypes are good for discussion: do we see angry or physically violent female characters? What happens to them? Or do women in literature more often express negative emotions through crying or sadness?

Normalising womanhood

Women are frequently the ones being marginalised. When they're not terrifyingly sexualised or infantilised, women are often historically written as magical beings, almost supernatural in their difference to men. The "Angel in the House" trope can be seen consistently throughout literature, written by men who profess to love women but keep them at a veiled distance. This lives on in the belief that men and women are somehow profoundly different and inexplicable to one another. Consider this quote from JK Rowling's *Harry Potter and the Order of the Phoenix*:

> *"'You should write a book,' Ron told Hermione as he cut up his potatoes, 'translating mad things girls do so boys can understand them.'"*

---

87. Tara M Chaplin, "Gender and emotion expression: a developmental contextual perspective", *Emotion Review*, 7:1, 2015

It's true that girls and boys can have radically different upbringings, and there are aspects of the male and female experiences that can be hard to understand, but that's what empathy is all about!

When tackling gender stereotypes it's easy to fall into the trap of positioning *everything* through a gendered lens, and I've certainly been guilty of that in the past. In an effort to teach a feminist curriculum, it can seem right to create units of women's writing or explore issues as they relate to women. But all this actually does is continue the separation of women. There's no such thing as "women's writing" – it's just *writing*. There's nothing wrong with issues-based teaching and it makes sense for many contexts, including non-fiction or poetry units. But let's make those units theme-, topic- or ideas-based, rather than gendered.

It's rare in most classrooms to give a piece of writing without any gender identification attached. Try giving a piece – fiction, non-fiction or poetry – to a class and asking them to consider it without any background information, including the author's name. Let the words speak for themselves. What do the students think are the important messages, ideas or phrases?

We might, then, choose to bring in some details. The writer was born in the 1850s. They're from Yorkshire. They're Muslim. Avoid pronouns. Let the students decide which details are relevant or not. If a detail *is* relevant, does it change their perspective on the poem? Why or why not? This is an interesting and relatively gentle way to start challenging some stereotypes, as well as being great practice for selective and purposeful use of context. For another interesting task, tell half the class that the writer is male and the other half that they're female – see what happens. The ensuing discussion often takes a different turn in each case, which can be extremely enlightening when you reveal the truth.

For this exercise, Imtiaz Dharker is an obvious poet to start with. She has so much seemingly contradictory context, which is another salient lesson – too often we expect writers' contexts to be simple and neat, fitting into little context boxes like those on an equality and diversity form. We also tend to think of writers' lives as unchanging and take little notice of where texts fall in the course of their life and literary experience.

Exploring language

As anyone who teaches A-level English language will know, language and gender is a fraught and fascinating topic. The research is often incredibly complex and contradictory, partly because it's so difficult to draw whole-gender conclusions when there are so many intersectional influences.

The inherent sexism of language needs to be explored and, happily for me, that goes hand in hand with a need to teach more linguistics in key stage 3. Since the removal of the spoken language controlled assessment, linguistics has taken a back seat to literature, but as far as gender is concerned it's a fascinating and fruitful topic to explore – one that all year groups can understand. A study of language and gender can be really interesting, allowing students to interrogate their own language use, as well as a great way to demonstrate much of the bias that exists around us.

A learning scheme on language and gender – Year 9	
Big questions • What influences the way people speak? • Is language gendered? • Do people change their language because of their gender? • Do men and women speak differently?	**Key vocabulary** Taboo, slur, sex, marked term, gender, idiolect, folk-linguistics
Success criteria Students can: • Explain some of the ways that language is gendered, especially taboo language. • Explain some of the contextual factors behind language use, including gender. • Undertake basic research into the topic and explain their findings in a tentative way.	**Home learning** Research project based on a topic linked to gender: • Ask people for five adjectives to describe something. Do women use more precise terms or a wider range? • Ask people for a list of 10 endearments they might use and compare the usage by gender, age and other contexts. • Ask a question, e.g. can you tell me about your day? Record the answer to discover whether women speak more than men.

Sample lesson ideas

Lesson		
Key question	Is language gendered?	**Resources**
Exploratory writing	Do you think men and women talk differently?	List of stereotypes about language and gender, e.g. women talk more, women use more words, men are more direct, men swear more, men interrupt more
Learning activities/ opportunities for writing and self-expression	• Using stereotype statements, discuss impressions and ideas – agree/disagree. • Explore words that are gendered, e.g. policeman. Are there more modern gender-neutral terms? Why/why not? • Explore words that originally had equal status but have undergone semantic derogation and changed meaning, e.g. master/mistress, governor/governess. • Using the statements, plan a piece of research to find out if men and women speak differently.	

Lesson		
Key question	What influences the way that individuals speak?	**Resources**
Exploratory talk	In groups that researched the same statement, share your findings. Explain whether you think gender made a difference and see if there are common conclusions.	British Library and BBC Voices project
Learning activities/ opportunities for writing and self-expression	• Listen to a couple of BBC Voices discussions of accent/dialect (from a range of regions). • Introduce idiolect and personal context – mind-map your own idiolect influences (with examples where possible of words/phrases). Are there words/phrases that you know you repeat regularly? • Read non-fiction extract on women apologising (or watch the Pantene "Sorry, Not Sorry" advert). • Writing: what is the effect of regularly saying sorry in this way? • Write a home-learning hypothesis: what has the most impact on people's idiolects?	

Lesson		
Key question	Do people change their language because of their gender?	**Resources** Home-learning research results
Exploratory writing	What did you discover?	
Exploratory talk	In groups that researched the same statement, share your findings. Explain whether you think gender made a difference and see if there are common conclusions.	
Learning activities/ opportunities for writing and self-expression	• Class discussion on the research findings. • Tabulating and interpreting data – working in trios to explore similarities/differences in the data. • Writing: from your data, explain what has the most influence on idiolect.	

Curriculum audit

A curriculum audit, focusing on gender and cultural background, is a great way to start interrogating the balance of the curriculum – and can be pretty surprising. Begin by listing the texts you currently teach and including some key information about them, e.g. the writer's era, gender and cultural background. It's staggering how a simple list of texts and writers can reveal a narrower curriculum than you might think. I also include the main character focus, to ensure that literary representations of women are balanced across the curriculum.

It's not about artificially creating balance – there's no requirement for a fifty-fifty split! But when so much popular, well-publicised and well-studied literature is by male authors, it will play into our decisions – and our expertise. Our own educational experiences could have been quite narrow, and it takes some time to address that through professional development focused on subject knowledge. But work of equal quality by women absolutely exists and we should be making use of it, seeking it out if necessary, to make it part of the future canon that our students consider.

Cultural capital is doubly empowering. We can teach students the "keys" to access hidden realms of power or understand commonly shared idioms, stories and references. We can also empower them all to experience a wider spectrum of cultures and draw new shared references, broadening the understanding of what currently exists. If we're teaching *The Odyssey*, can we add a page of Madeline Miller's *Circe* as well and discuss the perpetual resonance of Homer's epic? Or talk about the difficult decisions made by Emily Wilson as a female translator of the text?[88] Can we replace our Steinbeck with a Kate Chopin, a Charlotte Perkins Gilman or a Chimamanda Ngozi Adichie?

Era							
Characters focused on							
Cultural background							
Author gender							
Author							
Text							
Unit							
Year group							

88. Anna North, "Historically, men translated The Odyssey. Here's what happened when a woman took the job", *Vox*, 20 November 2017

- Does our English curriculum offer a balanced view of women and men, in characters and authors, across time periods and cultural backgrounds, and in all genres?
- Do students have opportunities to discuss a wide range of female characters?
- Do we talk about female characters in the context of women's history, thus developing a more subtle understanding?
- Do we avoid treating women as "other"? Are male and female writers side by side in the curriculum?
- Do we take opportunities to explore unconscious bias, e.g. bias created by sexism in language?
- Do we explore emotions and feelings in detail, giving students the vocabulary to express themselves thoughtfully and reflectively?
- Do we offer plenty of chances for students to practise empathy and compassion in the way they discuss characters and non-fiction texts?
- Do our non-fiction texts contribute to students' wider understanding of the political and social issues prevalent in their world?
- Are students encouraged to write regularly and expressively to find their own voice?

FURTHER RESOURCES

The Atlantic was founded in 1857 by Henry Wadsworth Longfellow, Ralph Waldo Emerson, James Russell Lowell and Harriet Beecher Stowe, among others. This magazine offers predominantly long-form journalism and is especially good for essay-style articles. It's often good for comparing with **The Guardian**, which is also freely available online. *theatlantic.com* and *theguardian.com*

Azeema is an annual print magazine and online platform that explores the lives of womxn (a term that explicitly includes transgender women) in the Middle East, North Africa, South Asia and beyond. *azeemamag.com*

British and Irish Women's Letters and Diaries is a searchable collection of 100,000 pages of diaries and letters from 500 women over 300 years. *bwld.alexanderstreet.com*

The British Library offers straightforward and accessible articles on gender and sexuality, particularly in the 19th century, and on Shakespeare and renaissance writers common at GCSE and A level. It also has digital collections of magazines and non-fiction resources linked to female life and representation. *bl.uk/romantics-and-victorians* and *bl.uk/shakespeare*

CommonLit is a website that provides multiple texts linked to novels and topics, organised by US grade levels. It also offers guided-reading, breaking-the-text-down and "read aloud" functions. *commonlit.org*

Feminist Review is a peer-reviewed journal that includes opinion essays, interviews and stories, as well as academic articles. *feminist-review.com*

gal-dem, an online and annually printed magazine, is committed to telling the stories of women and non-binary people of colour. *gal-dem.com*

James Clear has a selection of powerful speeches transcribed to download. *jamesclear.com/great-speeches*

Jezebel and Bitch: use these provocative online magazines with caution! They aim to provide a feminist response to the mainstream media. *jezebel.com* and *bitchmedia.org*

Mslexia publishes new writing by female authors and articles about women in the broad publishing industries, including online. *mslexia.co.uk*

Victorian Web has plenty of research articles on authors, politics and social issues (including gender) in the 19th century. There are links to non-fiction resources and it can be useful for finding related poetry by theme. *victorianweb.org*

6. STEM

Science and everyday life cannot and should
not be separated – Rosalind Franklin

I hadn't been aware that there were doors closed to
me until I started knocking on them – Gertrude B Elion

There's been a big drive in recent years to get girls into STEM, both in school and as careers. It's had mixed success. Numbers are going up – a bit. Women make up 54% of STEM postgraduates in the UK,[89] but this isn't replicated in the workforce. WISE, the campaign for gender balance in STEM, predicted that 1 million UK women would be working in core STEM job roles by 2020, with a "critical mass" of 30% female employment within reach in some roles.[90] Attitudes within and about STEM as a career option for women are still problematic. Almost any article about recruitment mentions the need for a culture of inclusion, and usually features stories of sexual harassment and women having to

---

89. "Minister calls to dispel girls' misconceptions of STEM subjects", Department for Education, 11 February 2019
90. "2018 workforce statistics", WISE, accessed 2019

"get on with it" and "enjoy the banter" (which is often at their expense). In short, women have to adapt to a traditionally masculine (and sexist) environment, but the hope is that a critical mass of female employment will begin to dilute this potentially toxic culture.

Inclusive workplaces are successful in every industry. Research by Deloitte shows that when employees feel their environments are inclusive and diverse, their ability to innovate rises by 80%.[91] This is unsurprising when you consider that innovation requires confidence, security and the ability to take risks without repercussions. Diversity (of gender and ethnicity) boosts creativity, problem-solving, lateral thinking, commitment and motivation, creating a more flexible workplace and increasing profitability.[92] It seems a promising virtuous cycle: greater diversity leads to a more enjoyable and productive workplace, which in turn becomes more inclusive and welcoming. Employers are increasingly keen to build on this.

In secondary schools, the number of girls taking STEM A levels has increased by 26% since 2010. But, strangely, they're less likely than boys to see them as useful when getting a job and far less likely to consider a STEM subject their favourite. Interestingly, maths was the most common answer among boys when asked which area of study was most likely to lead to a job, while English was the most popular answer among girls. Science was the most common answer among boys *and* girls when asked which subject would yield the highest salary.[93] A survey of young people in the UK found that one reason girls dismissed a STEM career was that they felt these jobs lacked creativity, with just 32% associating STEM careers with being creative.[94]

The statistics hide some pretty big variations, with girls particularly under-represented in engineering, computing and physics. Girls are

91. Research by Deloitte quoted in *Creating Cultures Where All Engineers Thrive: a unique study of inclusion across UK engineering*, Royal Academy of Engineering, 2017

92. *Delivering Through Diversity*, McKinsey & Company, January 2018

93. *Attitudes Towards STEM Subjects by Gender at KS4*, Department for Education, February 2019

94. "Accenture survey points to untapped opportunity for girls to fulfill their creative aspirations with STEM careers", Accenture, 14 March 2018

more likely to opt for biology and maths, yet they outperform boys in all STEM subjects.[95] Wider industry statistics show a similarly stark disparity between disciplines: 12% of engineers are female, compared with 43% of science professionals (and even that masks a difference between chemical, biological and physical sciences).

A note of caution: it's important not to overestimate the significance of STEM in the curriculum. No doubt, it's important. But so are all the other subjects – and every single one can lead to potentially lucrative careers, if that's our end goal with education. If we push STEM too hard, we risk alienating students. After all, this is about empowering young people with that most feminist of things: choice. And because the STEM curriculum covers such a wide range of subjects and career paths, ideas within it need to be presented carefully.

Is computing a man's game?

When it comes to changing the narrative around STEM, the history of computing provides an extremely interesting opportunity. It demonstrates the importance of early intervention to ensure interest and access.

In the 1950s, women were actively encouraged to become software programmers, possibly because the computing industry perceived hardware as more prestigious and exciting, so software was relegated to a female occupation. Following on from many women's work in codebreaking during the Second World War, it was believed that women had the logical, meticulous natures needed for the task.[96] In 1967, a *Cosmopolitan* article reported that women could make US$20,000 a year (equivalent to US$150,000 today), which was even more impressive considering how few professional, highly trained jobs were available to women with maths degrees.

But in the 1980s, women's participation in computer and information science degrees in the US began to decline, and a study found that early

95. *Attitudes Towards STEM Subjects by Gender at KS4*, Department for Education, February 2019

96. Clive Thompson, "The secret history of women in coding", *The New York Times Magazine*, 13 February 2019

exposure to computing was the key: boys arriving at university had already had personal computers and been given the freedom to work and play on them.[97] Fathers were more engaged with technology than mothers, and there was an increasing perception that if you hadn't been single-mindedly working on computing while at high school, you weren't "a real programmer". Women said they felt judged for not being "hard core" enough and having other interests, which sometimes led to their dropping out or changing degrees. By the end of the 1980s, the popular perception of the white male programmer was set.[98] And now, the computing industry is spending millions of dollars on trying to redress the gender balance and eradicating the endemic sexism that women face.

Leading improvement

So, what can we do to increase students' engagement with STEM and boost post-16 uptake among girls in particular? Here are five key areas that I'll go on to explore in further detail.

- **Limit unconscious bias among teachers and students.** A study by King's College London has found that entry to science A levels is more tightly restricted than other subjects and the perception of "science for the brainy" could put students off. This disproportionately affects girls, especially those who define themselves as "highly feminine" – they are particularly unlikely to aspire to scientific careers because being intelligent is often perceived as contrary to being feminine. Teachers, too, demonstrate bias against girls in science.[99]
- **Shift the focus of intervention from "increasing interest" to "building science capital".** Many interventions are focused

---

97. Jane Margolis and Allan Fisher, *Unlocking the Clubhouse: women in computing*, MIT Press, 2001
98. Clive Thompson, "The secret history of women in coding", *The New York Times Magazine*, 13 February 2019
99. *ASPIRES: young people's science and career aspirations, age 10-14*, King's College London, 2013

on sparking interest in science, but research suggests the most effective way to improve scientific aspiration and post-16 uptake is to cultivate students' scientific capital, making science a part of everyday life rather than something "done by experts".[100]

- **Improve careers education related to STEM.** Demonstrating a range of career options beyond the laboratory (the common image associated with "science careers") can help students to see the relevance and purpose of STEM.

- **Promote the creativity of STEM subjects.** This is often seriously underestimated by students – many STEM careers are highly creative, but in schools the emphasis can be on the "right" answers, the carefully defined mark scheme and the correct way to do experiments. This focus on "right" can deter students who feel they can't demonstrate these qualities (perfectionism again) or those who value a more interpretive approach.

- **Start early.** Really successful intervention needs to start in primary schools. Good science teaching is essential, but partnerships with local secondaries can also be really helpful.

Unconscious bias

Unconscious bias and perceptions of gender are huge issues in the classroom, as research from the Institute of Physics (IOP) confirms. It found that girls were two and a half times more likely to study A-level physics if they attended a girls' school rather than a co-ed school, which suggests the issue is not that girls aren't fundamentally (or biologically!) suited to science.[101] This isn't as pronounced in other STEM subjects, but research shows that it's girls' perceptions of themselves in relation to boys that are holding them back, exacerbated by teacher bias or a prevailing view in school of STEM subjects as "too hard". Another IOP study found, for example, that teachers reported

---

100. Ibid.
101. *It's Different for Girls: the influence of schools*, Institute of Physics, October 2012

these as curriculum areas that only girls would find difficult,[102] as well as commenting that girls were less confident and didn't participate in discussion as much as boys.

This suggests that teachers may be limiting their students through unconscious bias; 67% admitted to some stereotypes about gender and STEM, and 40% thought gender biases around STEM had been established by the end of primary school.[103] In many cases, simply becoming aware of bias can be enough to remedy it.[104] But some unconscious biases are deeply implicit and contradict an individual's openly held and *consciously* practised beliefs. In our schools, we can use data as a starting point to explore whether gender gaps exist in the following areas:

- In the take-up of STEM subjects at GCSE and A level.
- In attainment across the key stages.
- In participation in lessons.
- In who is being asked questions, and what kind of questions.
- In extracurricular club participation.
- In post-school destinations.

The messages students are given at school and at home about the difficulty of STEM have a huge impact. It is crucial to hammer home the message that girls and boys are of equal ability. Telling women that the results of maths tests show gender differences actually makes women perform worse in such tests, likely because there is such a strong systemic social correlation of femaleness with poor mathematical ability.[105] We

102. *Girls in the Physics Classroom: a review of the research on the participation of girls in physics,* Institute of Physics, June 2006

103. "Accenture survey points to untapped opportunity for girls to fulfill their creative aspirations with STEM careers", Accenture, 14 March 2018

104. Nilanjana Dasgupta and Anthony G Greenwald, "On the malleability of automatic attitudes: combating automatic prejudice with images of admired and disliked individuals", *Journal of Personality and Social Psychology,* 81:5, 2001

105. Steven J Spencer, Claude M Steele and Diane M Quinn, "Stereotype threat and women's math performance", *Journal of Experimental Social Psychology,* 35:1, January 1999

have a lot of time and social pressure to make up for when it comes to ensuring that women feel confident in STEM subjects.

The language we use to talk *about* subjects matters as much as the language used *in* subjects. When examples of "difficult" subjects are given, is it always science and maths? If teachers and parents sympathise by saying, "I was never any good at maths either," it legitimises a student's feeling that they're "not a maths person" and tacitly advocates giving up. After all, if they'll never be any good at it, why not spend their time on something more enjoyable and comfortable? A more conscious awareness of how we talk about such subjects has to be part of our whole-school approach to STEM.

Science capital

Research shows that the more science capital a young person has, the more likely they are to want to continue with their science education.[106] Making science an everyday experience, while capturing the wonder and awe, is an incredible skill and the most likely way to break down barriers of social attitudes and expectations towards science. Rather than seeing science as "for scientists", students have to see science as "for me" and "for everyone". Science is part of every single aspect of life – harnessing the society and environment around us is a powerful way to send the message to students that science is not only relevant to them, but also essential and exciting.

Research suggests there are many factors that affect science capital:

- Scientific literacy – knowing how science works and how to apply this to daily life.
- Science-related preferences, such as social valuing of science.
- Knowledge about the transferable skills of science into work, and the extrinsic value of science qualifications.
- Consuming science-related media including TV, books and online content.

---

106. *Science Capital Made Clear,* King's College London, 2016

- Participation in out-of-school science learning, e.g. clubs and museums.
- Family scientific knowledge and qualifications.
- Knowing people in science-related jobs.
- Talking to others outside school about science.[107]

So, what can teachers do to build students' science capital?

- **Create extracurricular opportunities** such as STEM clubs or participation in science awards like CREST. Use STEM clubs as a way to bring more hands-on experiences to science. Give students a focus for half a term – for example, participating in a national project that explores the decline or growth of certain species.[108] Or perhaps they could meet a climatologist and then spend the year working on climate-related issues within school.
- **Take an elicit-value-link approach to lessons.** "Elicit" is about drawing out current knowledge, experience and interests. "Value" is recognising students' current ways of being, with discussion about their knowledge and the relevance of science to their lives. Then "link" this expertise to the more precise or canonical knowledge, to develop it further. This personalises science in a way that textbooks simply can't and makes it more relevant. It also makes the canonical knowledge more accessible because it builds on a common understanding. We do a lot of this implicitly, but the "elicit" stage is critical in developing an emotional connection with science.[109]
- **Run a science fair**, like the Big Bang Fair, and bring in industry experts to feed back to students.[110]

107. Effrosyni Nomikou, Louise Archer and Heather King, "Building 'science capital' in the classroom", *School Science Review,* 98, 2017

108. Lynn Nickerson, "The wonders of science clubs", British Science Association, accessed 2019

109. Effrosyni Nomikou, Louise Archer and Heather King, "Building 'science capital' in the classroom", *School Science Review,* 98, 2017

110. thebigbangfair.co.uk

- **Run a project across multiple half-terms** so students can see the progress they make. Then deliver a presentation or celebration event on their findings, so they understand the process of research and dissemination.
- **Link science to the everyday** and contextualise learning.
- **Embrace learning for its own sake.** We study science to understand the magic and beauty of the world around us, not to condense it into an eight-mark question. Until it's necessary to practise exam technique, use other forms of assessment that are more closely aligned with the day-to-day reality of those working in science.
- **Do more practical investigations.** In a Wellcome Trust survey, 29% of GCSE students reported doing practical science less than once a month.[111]
- **Introduce science ambassadors**, working with peers within school and feeder primaries, to foster a culture of positivity around STEM education, as well as building students' confidence in their ability.[112] Students can take a range of roles, including mentoring younger pupils and creating STEM days for feeder primaries, organising activities for taster days or setting up a science fair. In lessons, they can be the "go-to" person for support and revision guidance, or be asked to create revision resources.
- **Broaden the understanding of what "science" is.** Spend some time with students thinking about where science fits into their lives. Make explicit links to the role that science plays. A "science diary" can be an interesting way to do this: for a day, students should record the impact that science has on their life. Everything is fair game, from their phone alarm waking them up in the morning to opening the fridge to get a drink, getting the bus to school, the weather, the environment, recycling,

111. *Young People's Views on Science Education: Science Education Tracker research report*, Wellcome Trust, February 2017

112. *Improving Gender Balance: reflections on the impact of interventions in schools*, Institute of Physics, March 2017

gravity and the stars. Then get them to think about the processes involved (this will require more input before they've studied these processes, but here's where a broad overview of the curriculum might be useful). Some students might need a primer as a starting point.[113]

- **Cultivate parental engagement in science**, through a combination of passive methods (regular newsletter updates) and active ones (asking students to debate an issue at home, inviting parents into taster lessons, a game night that involves science).
- **Work with other subjects to create science capital**, e.g. through English non-fiction or history topics.

The enormous breadth of the science curriculum can sometimes mean we get tunnel vision, panicked that we haven't enough time to cover all the content. But if we review that content and focus on making concrete connections to the world around us, then students are more likely to engage holistically with science and really understand its value.

Careers education

This is part of improving science capital and of encouraging students to see themselves in a science career. We can take a much broader view of what "science careers" can be, looking beyond the stereotypical researcher, doctor or astronaut.

Develop whole-school activities – for example, events like International Women in Engineering Day (23 June). Most sizeable companies have outreach and education programmes that specifically aim to boost women's participation in STEM; they will be able to provide speakers or resources to support you. Several of the organisations listed at the end of this chapter are able to connect teachers with STEM professionals who can speak to students, provide judging for events, or work with groups on small projects.

113. "What has science done for you lately?", *Understanding Science*, University of California Museum of Paleontology, accessed 2019

Skipton Girls' High School runs a Water Week, for example, during which students hear a presentation from the local company JN Bentley on its work in the civil engineering and environmental sector, as well as from Yorkshire Water on its partner charity WaterAid. Over several days, the students work on projects connected with water conservation, technology and charity, and they participate in a sponsored walk to the local reservoir to raise money for WaterAid. At the end of the week, the students present their work as a formal pitch to the company.

The Gatsby benchmarks of good careers guidance require encounters with employers, employees and workplaces, and recommend that curriculum learning is linked to careers. Educational visits, therefore, could involve trips to local organisations, where students can witness first-hand the wide range of STEM-related career options.

Creativity in STEM

Coding is taught throughout the national curriculum, so it's essential that we make the most of this opportunity. We need to capture the magic and creativity of STEM subjects like computing and encourage students to see the possibilities. Coding is a chance for boys and girls to explore the logical puzzle-solving and creative nature of programming. It involves literally making something from nothing – it's astonishing how a totally immersive experience can begin with just a few words on a screen.

There has been an explosion in educational STEM kits and competitions, like the FIRST Lego League,[114] the Tomorrow's Engineers EEP Robotics Challenge[115] and the School Robot Competition.[116] Money is undoubtedly a factor here, for materials and registration fees, but many competitions do offer some support to disadvantaged students, or local companies might be keen to sponsor entries as part of their educational outreach programmes.

114. education.theiet.org/first-lego-league-programmes
115. robotics.tomorrowsengineers.org.uk
116. ukras.org/school-robot-competition

Early intervention

Intervention needs to start in primary schools. Primaries are usually much better than secondaries at getting out and exploring science! Children find minibeasts, grow plants, hatch chickens, watch caterpillars become butterflies, or experiment with different combinations of liquids and solids. Cooking also offers great potential for scientific exploration. The starting point is relevance to children's lives – *then* you can make it clear that this is biology, chemistry or physics. Sometimes children don't realise that all this wonder comes from science.[117]

Good science teaching is essential, but partnerships with local secondaries can also be really helpful – secondary science ambassadors can work with primary students to inspire and encourage them. It can also help secondaries to know what their students have done at primary school and whether they need to make their science more challenging.

Auditing the curriculum

Just as in other subjects, the textbooks and resources used in science are critical in confirming or challenging gender stereotypes. A 2015 study of key stage 3 science textbooks, for example, found significant gender bias. They used "more male images, more male role models, more male pronouns, more male-gendered words" and showed men in higher status roles than women.[118] The same study found that Rosalind Franklin and Marie Curie were the only named female scientists and the narratives surrounding them discussed their achievements in light of the male scientists they worked with.

Most new specifications and textbooks for A level and GCSE are quite good when it comes to bias: examination papers tend to use "person" or "student" and opt for gender-neutral pronouns. Many recent books produced by exam boards, if they use examples and photographs, aim for balance and avoid always portraying men hard at work in the

117. *'State of the Nation' Report of UK Primary Science Education*, Wellcome Trust, September 2017

118. Claire L Parkin and Sharron Mackenzie, "Is there gender bias in key stage 3 science textbooks?", *The Advanced Journal of Professional Practice* 1:1, November 2017

lab while women sit passively in front of a computer. However, this isn't universal and budget challenges often mean that, in practice, KS3 textbooks aren't replaced, particularly if a department has had to replace KS4 or KS5 textbooks in light of the new specifications.

Library budget cuts exacerbate the problem. Children's non-fiction on science across the age ranges is plagued with gender bias. Women are depicted as "passive, lower status and unskilled", and become increasingly under-depicted as the target age of books increases.[119]

A study of US magazines published between 1910 and 1955 found:

> *"No woman, either scientist or journalist, was listed as the author of an article on mathematics, astronomy, archaeology, or paleontology, despite the fact that women were actively engaged in research in those fields. Women authors tended to write about research in the social or biological sciences ... but were much less visible as authors of articles on physics or chemistry."*[120]

In many respects this hasn't changed much – male portrayals of scientists in television programmes still significantly outweigh female portrayals.[121] In science books for children, women are portrayed as less active and more static; men are more likely to be depicted actually doing experiments, while women are portrayed as assistants.[122]

A detailed study of the representation of astronauts and doctors in 20th-century children's books found that male pronouns were used

---

119. Claire L Parkin and Sharron Mackenzie, "Is there gender bias in key stage 3 science textbooks?", *The Advanced Journal of Professional Practice* 1:1, November 2017

120. Marcel C LaFollette, "Eyes on the stars: images of women scientists in popular magazines", *Science, Technology, and Human Values*, 13:3, 1988

121. Marilee Long, Jocelyn Steinke, Brooks Applegate, Maria Knight Lapinski, Marne J Johnson and Sayani Ghosh, "Portrayals of male and female scientists in television programs popular among middle school-age children", *Science Communication*, 32:3, December 2010

122. Elizabeth F Caldwell and Susan Wilbraham, "Hairdressing in space: depiction of gender in science books for children", *Journal of Science and Popular Culture*, 1:2, September 2018

almost exclusively. Even when an accompanying photograph was of the NASA astronaut Sunita Williams, her name wasn't used and, even worse, the pronoun was male, leading to what researchers called a "symbolic annihilation" of women.[123] When female astronauts *were* pictured, they weren't driving shuttles, doing experiments or space-walking. Representations of doctors, however, were more gender-balanced, reflecting a greater acceptance of women in medical professions. More recent books, like Rachel Ignotofsky's beautiful *Women in Science: 50 fearless pioneers who changed the world*, are combating gender stereotypes, but school budgets often mean that newer titles are limited in libraries.

Beyond the textbooks that support the curriculum, scientific non-fiction has an important role to play, as few young people have opportunities to go inside laboratories or meet astronauts. Books are a major source of information, teaching children about people and places beyond their everyday experiences.[124]

Auditing scientific non-fiction

Elizabeth F Caldwell and Susan Wilbraham's study of gender depictions in children's science books[125] includes some useful questions to consider when auditing the non-fiction available to students:

- Are women positioned prominently or in the background?
- Are women younger?
- Do captions or text use sexist language, e.g. "men" rather than "people"?

123. Janice McCabe, Emily Fairchild, Liz Grauerholz, Bernice A Pescosolido and Daniel Tope, "Gender in twentieth-century children's books: patterns of disparity in titles and central characters", *Gender and Society*, 25:2, April 2011

124. Sharyl Bender Peterson and Mary Alyce Lach, "Gender stereotypes in children's books: their prevalence and influence on cognitive and affective development", *Gender and Education*, 2:2, 1990

125. Elizabeth F Caldwell and Susan Wilbraham, "Hairdressing in space: depiction of gender in science books for children", *Journal of Science and Popular Culture*, 1:2, September 2018

- Are men pictured in lower-status jobs than women?
- Are men and women performing the same job equally?
- If the book is mainly about an occupation, is there an overall sense that men and women are just as likely to do it?
- If the occupation is traditionally gendered (e.g. nurse) are there instances where the other gender is portrayed?
- What are the doctors, engineers or astronauts doing in the pictures?
- Are women as likely to be doing a particular activity?
- What is the activity level: static/busy/active?
- Are women doing less exciting or dangerous tasks (e.g. administration, rather than surgery or piloting a space shuttle)?
- Is one person serving or caring for another?
- Where are the professionals located?
- Are they in places reserved for that occupation (e.g. space station, operating theatre) or in places open to the general public (e.g. waiting rooms)?
- What are the doctors or astronauts holding, or immediately next to?
- Are women associated with smaller objects?
- Are women as likely to be wearing the stereotypical "uniform" of the job (e.g. white coat, spacesuit)?
- Do women have long hair?
- Do women wear trousers?
- Are men dressed more formally?

- Do we offer creative opportunities for students to design and lead their own projects in computing and science?
- Have we explored the possibility of unconscious bias in our teaching, including question-targeting and attitudes in lessons?
- Have we audited textbooks and teaching resources for gender bias?
- Have we checked whole-school materials for gender bias in relation to STEM?
- Do we promote clear and broad ideas about career pathways related to STEM?
- Do students have extracurricular opportunities to explore STEM further, including clubs, visits and workplace-related experiences?
- Do we have a parental engagement programme that encourages families to talk about STEM and enjoy experimenting with it?
- Do we have a programme of speakers/support from local business enterprises, reflecting a range of genders and occupations?
- Do we work with other subjects to create cross-curricular science capital?
- Are there regular events and opportunities related to STEM?

FURTHER RESOURCES

Arkwright Engineering Scholarships allow students to be sponsored by commercial organisations or charities, receiving hands-on experience and a mentor for career planning. *arkwright.org.uk*

The British Science Association runs the Youth Industrial Strategy Competition for 11- to 19-year-olds and the CREST Awards (similar to the Arts Award). *www.britishscienceassociation.org*

The Institute of Physics offers teaching resources and CPD support, as well as teaching and learning coaches who work with partner schools, funded by the Department for Education. *iop.org*

The Royal Society of Chemistry runs an annual UK Chemistry Olympiad and has regional education coordinators to offer in-school support and CPD. *rsc.org/campaigning-outreach/outreach*

Skype a Scientist connects classrooms with scientists around the world, allowing students to witness science in action. *skypeascientist.com*

STEM Learning has active forums on its website, offering support for activity ideas and outreach or ambassador programmes. Ambassadors can speak to or visit your STEM club. *stem.org.uk*

The Women's Engineering Society organises competitions for primary and secondary students and has regional coordinators. *wes.org.uk*

7. Languages

The limits of my language mean the limits
of my world – Ludwig Wittgenstein

Languages are seen by students as being on the "feminine" side of the curriculum, which could contribute to their being considered less important and prestigious.[126] This "feminine" reputation perhaps comes from the intense amount of conversation and oral practice required, as well as stereotypes of girls' superior communication skills. Languages also have the reputation of being harder, perhaps linked with a wider (white) British monolingualism and the perception that learning the vocabulary of another language is tougher than learning the content of other subjects. Continued efforts by, among others, the UK government and the British Council to promote language learning in schools focus on extrinsic rather than intrinsic motivations. But girls *are* interested in language learning:

"Girls consistently appear more interested in the study of a foreign language than boys, and manifest an evident liking for the culture, the country and the speakers of

126. Becky Francis, "The gendered subject: students' subject preferences and discussions of gender and subject ability", *Oxford Review of Education*, 26:1, 2000

that language. Whereas boys' reasons for studying the language are mainly instrumental, girls' motivations tend to be integrative."[127]

The same study also suggests that "sex-stereotyping of jobs in society endorses language learning as an accomplishment ... [Girls] are generally more inclined to believe that language will be useful to them in their future careers." The word "accomplishment" here is an interesting one: French has been on the list of necessary "accomplishments" for refined young women for centuries, long before careers were a consideration for female education. Placing French and Italian alongside activities such as music, singing, dancing and needlework gives the impression that these languages are easier (easy enough for a woman to learn without becoming a bluestocking or educated to an unseemly degree) and less suitable for boys. Young men may have learned French, but the Latin and Greek of a classical education were considered more academic and prestigious. Although French, German and Spanish gained status during the 19th century, this occurred alongside an influx of female teachers and students into education. Perhaps some of the perceptions of modern foreign languages as more feminine are in fact a hangover from this idea of "masculine" versus "feminine" languages?

The extrinsic value of language learning – primarily, career options and financial reward – appear diminished in light of the UK's changing relationship with the EU. The messages students see in the media about reduced employment opportunities in Europe, as well as their own experiences, tell them that most people they will be connected with will speak English. It's promising for the continued uptake of MFL, then, that girls' motivation is more intrinsic and integrative.[128] Ironically, though, this might contribute to a reduction in status: when the emphasis of

---

127. Paula López-Rúa, "The sex variable in foreign language learning: an integrative approach", *Porta Linguarum*, January 2006

128. Marion Williams, Robert Burden and Ursula Lanvers, "'French is the language of love and stuff': student perceptions of issues related to motivation in learning a foreign language", *British Educational Research Journal*, 28:4, August 2002

education shifts towards preparation for work and employment, MFL can take a hit.

Girls and MFL

Girls aren't naturally better at learning languages than boys, but some studies suggest they have different strategies, including using a wider range of skills and study methods. There are also fairly widespread perceptions that language learners are high achievers, but there's not a lot of research to support a theory of "natural" intelligence in languages. What seems more likely is that successful language learners are good at absorbing content (grammar and vocabulary) and can transfer those skills into content learning for other subjects.[129]

The government's ambition is to achieve the Teaching Schools Council recommendation for the vast majority of pupils to take a GCSE in a modern foreign language,[130] and is seeking to develop language hubs across England focusing on Spanish, French and German.[131] Currently, there is a significant difference in entry when it comes to gender: more girls take French, German and Spanish at GCSE and A level (nearly twice as many in some A levels) and achieve more highly. Yet this doesn't reflect the substantial decline in uptake across both genders, as most MFL teachers are painfully aware. GCSEs in French and German have declined by 30% in five years in England, with Spanish relatively stable at a 2% decline but still far below French in uptake. Arabic, Chinese, Polish and modern Hebrew have grown by more than 10%, which might suggest more students are being encouraged to take GCSEs in their first languages, particularly as they often count in the "languages" section of the English Baccalaureate. At A level,

129. Paula López-Rúa, "The sex variable in foreign language learning: an integrative approach", *Porta Linguarum*, January 2006
130. Ian Bauckham, *Modern Foreign Languages Pedagogy Review,* Teaching Schools Council, 2016
131. "Languages boost to deliver skilled workforce for UK's businesses", Department for Education, 3 August 2018

French and German continue to decline, while Spanish is holding relatively steady.[132]

In creating a more feminist education – one that values communication and collaboration – languages play a central role. Skills gained through language learning include improved confidence in speaking, resilience when faced with challenge, and the empathy that comes from exploring another culture through its language (never mind the benefit of knowing another language for its own sake and the contribution that language learning can make to one's understanding of English). Bringing some of these skills to the forefront in language lessons can help to consciously develop them across the curriculum.

Curriculum choices

Most MFL curricula focus on culturally relevant topics: education, holidays or, by A level, specific aspects of arts and literature. Content and teaching materials can be usefully examined to see whether they develop or challenge gender stereotypes, and whether they are interesting and stimulating enough to enthuse and encourage students, broadening their horizons.[133] As with STEM, it's important to make consistent extrinsic and intrinsic links to the value of MFL, ensuring that young people see languages as providing concrete work-related skills, as well as more abstract gains in empathy and communication.

Translation, required in the new GCSEs, is a valuable working skill and often a key requirement of professional linguists. It encourages students to be precise, paying attention to detail and nuance, as well as providing opportunities to assess spelling, vocabulary, grammar, phrases and cultural references.

Play and creativity with language can be a great way to make students, girls *and* boys, more invested in the intrinsic rewards of language learning – other benefits include increased confidence in writing and

---

132. Teresa Tinsley, *Language Trends 2019: language teaching in primary and secondary schools in England – survey report*, British Council, 2019

133. Ian Bauckham, *Modern Foreign Languages Pedagogy Review*, Teaching Schools Council, 2016

oracy skills in particular. Writing children's books, singing songs and learning everyday skills are all ways to make language learning more playful and meaningful.

Oracy focus

Most of what I discussed in the chapter on oracy applies here. Languages offer an extraordinary opportunity to promote girls' speaking abilities and build their confidence. After all, if they can speak and be understood in a non-native language, what could they accomplish in their own? The best language teachers spend as much time speaking in the target language as possible and, when it comes to oracy, a confident, encouraging and playful approach is usually most beneficial. The ideal way to promote spoken confidence is to give students plenty of scope to experiment with language and to hear it being spoken, by themselves and by others.

Exploratory talk is critical. When students have the chance to explore language itself, reaching for phrases beyond their current understanding and experimenting with grammar until they find the right solution, they gain a deeper understanding of the way the language works, as well as its relationship with (and difference to) their own.

Language and gender bias

Through the study of modern languages, we can interrogate how the words we use shape our perceptions of the world around us. One study, for example, explored grammatical gender. In Spanish, "bridge" is a masculine noun, while in German it's feminine. Spanish speakers described bridges as strong, sturdy and towering, while German speakers referred to them as beautiful, elegant, fragile and pretty. "Keys" is a masculine word in Germany, where they were described as hard, heavy and useful; in Spain, where "keys" is a feminine word, they were characterised as intricate, little, lovely and tiny.[134]

---

134. Lera Boroditsky, Lauren A Schmidt and Webb Phillips, "Sex, syntax, and semantics" in *Language in Mind: advances in the study of language and cognition*, ed. D Gentner and S Goldin-Meadow, Cambridge University Press, 2003

Explicitly discussing some of these connotations reveals the gendered nature of the English language, too, and the way that so many of the words we use create implicit understandings without our being aware. Developing that conscious awareness is the first step towards addressing and changing such perceptions.

- Is there a gender gap in languages results across the school?
- Are any gender gaps similar in different languages?
- What is the reputation and status of languages in the school?
- Who are the speakers in listening tests, and are they speaking without gender bias?
- Do textbooks and other resources challenge gender stereotypes?
- Do students regularly celebrate other languages – for example, participating in the European Day of Languages or saluting their own variety of languages?
- Which languages are taught in the school and why? How was this decided and when?
- What motivates students to study a language at GCSE? How can teachers harness extrinsic and intrinsic motivating factors to support language learning?
- Do students explore the cultural aspects of languages – for example, through foreign film clubs, reading or music?
- Does the school library include foreign-language books of familiar texts to support students' vocabulary development?

FURTHER RESOURCES

The British Council offers support in employing modern language assistants who are native speakers of languages including French, Spanish, German and Mandarin. *britishcouncil.org*

The Teaching Schools Council's *Modern Foreign Languages Pedagogy Review* offers recommendations on language teaching, curriculum and assessment. *tscouncil.org.uk*

8. Physical education

I've learned to love my muscles a lot more than when I was younger, because I got made fun of a lot for them … I wish I could tell my younger self to be positive about my body, because when you learn to love your body, you learn to fall in love with yourself – Simone Biles

I didn't want to lift weights. I really avoided those exercises for a while, but it was something I had to make a big decision on. You can't become Olympic champion or world champion without having a strength-conditioning programme. I had to realise there was a bigger picture – Jessica Ennis-Hill

"Fat is a feminist issue," declared the psychotherapist Susie Orbach in 1978. More than 40 years later, women and girls are still locked in a struggle over body image, body confidence and fitness.

According to a report by Women in Sport (formerly the Women's Sport and Fitness Foundation), only 12% of 14-year-old girls meet the guidelines for physical activity in and out of school, around half the number of boys the same age.[135] Research has found that the decline begins before secondary school, but becomes most pronounced in Years 8 and 9. Yet Women in Sport also found that girls want to be more active – they know exercise is important and good for them. We have a responsibility to bridge the divide between girls' desires and their behaviours, and to understand the reasons why they don't get involved in sport.

PE requires that girls focus on their bodies in a mindful and positive way: how to move, how to react, how to develop strength, stamina and coordination. Meanwhile, social messages scream at girls, "Don't move too much!", "Don't take up space!", "Keep control!". These messages tell them that their bodies are imperfect and need to be improved, but only when it comes to appearance. Although there is an online movement to suggest that "strong is sexy", it hasn't permeated mainstream discussions of fitness and is built on the idea that women's bodies are of most value when they are attractive.

Social messages about sport are complex and many still focus on exercise as a fast route to feminine stereotypes. The sports writer Anna Kessel has identified some of the problems:

> "Women are told that being physically active is all about hard work, about getting the perfect body. Shifting that baby fat. We are not told we might have fun running about, chucking a ball, leaping into the air."[136]

As I discussed earlier, plenty of biological myth surrounds the assessment of women's relative strength, but among those teenage girls and boys who aren't training to be world-class athletes, the differences are less than we might think. Relative size and power might be the most visual differences between boys and girls, among older students particularly, but for most of their school careers are these always

---

135. *Changing the Game, for Girls*, Women's Sport and Fitness Foundation, 2012
136. Anna Kessel, "Let's get physical: how women's sport can conquer body image", *The Guardian*, 12 June 2016

very pronounced? With training, both sexes can radically alter their physicality, if they so wish.

It's not girls' lack of ability that prevents their full participation in sport. The achievements of female athletes challenge the biological argument even further. Serena Williams might be the highest profile woman to compete while pregnant, winning the Australian Open in 2017, but she's far from the only one. Pregnant speed skaters, canoeists, volleyballers and snowboarders have competed in the Olympics since 1920, when Magda Julin won the figure-skating gold medal while three months pregnant.[137] In schools, it's usually factors other than physical capability that hold girls back when it comes to PE.

Sport in schools

Access to sport in UK schools is generally pretty good and it improved with the legacy of the 2012 London Olympics. The statutory curriculum requires students to develop techniques and performance in competitive sports, dance and outdoor activities. A 2013 Ofsted report suggested that, on average, schools provided two hours of PE a week, including sport, dance, athletics and swimming, as well as extracurricular clubs.[138] Yet provision varies significantly with age. It often drops to about 90 minutes in KS4 and to an average of just 34 minutes in KS5, when PE is no longer compulsory. Secondary PE seems to be decreasing year on year for both genders, something teachers have attributed in large part to an increasing EBacc focus in schools.[139] They also point out that there's a comparative drop in funding at secondary level, which means much of the good work done at primary is undone. Of course, this is also the time when puberty and adolescence can shake student confidence and identity.

In primary schools, the picture is broadly gender-positive for the kind of activities on offer. Boys and girls are often taught together and

137. "Olympians who competed while pregnant", sport-reference.com, accessed 2019

138. *Beyond 2012: outstanding physical education for all*, Ofsted, 2013

139. *PE Provision in Secondary Schools 2018: survey research report*, Youth Sport Trust, February 2018

make similar progress.[140] Primary schools do benefit – at the moment – from additional ring-fenced sports funding.[141] Schools have to report how they spend this money, just as they do their academic pupil premium: primary school records reveal a vast variety of external coaches and activities including skateboarding, cycling, swimming, aerobics, yoga, orienteering and karate. They use the money to hire facilities, pay professionals and buy equipment.

In secondary school, boys begin to outperform girls in practical PE lessons. They "tend to dominate in practical activities" and are more likely to opt for GCSE PE (again getting lower grades on average).[142] This might reflect the fact that secondary PE appears to be a very different creature. For one thing, boys and girls are taught separately more often than at primary school; *TES* regularly features adverts for "teachers of girls' PE" and "teachers of boys' PE". The Equality Act 2010 prohibits segregation of children's PE classes based on ethnicity, but allows gender separation:

> *"A 'gender-affected activity' is a sport, game or other activity of a competitive nature in circumstances where the physical strength, stamina or physique of the average girl (or boy) would put her (or him) at a disadvantage in competition with the average boy (or girl) … The judgment on whether girls would be at a physical disadvantage needs to take into account the particular group in question, so it is much less likely to justify separation in relation to sports for younger children."*[143]

Schools have to provide "comparable sporting activities" and can't treat them less favourably – for example, providing better resources to one

---

140. *Evidence on Physical Education and Sport in Schools,* Department for Education, 5 August 2013

141. *PE and Sport Premium: conditions of grant 2019 to 2020,* Department for Education, 2019

142. *Beyond 2012: outstanding physical education for all,* Ofsted, 2013

143. *Gender Separation in Mixed Schools: non-statutory guidance,* Department for Education, June 2018

team over another. I explored the available curricula in several schools and found a fairly traditional mix in many of them. Girls play netball, hockey and rounders, while boys play rugby and football. Athletics is fairly common to both, as is cross-country running. Photographs show a similarly gendered approach, with all-male or all-female teams.

In some respects this is a response to county-wide competitions' single-gender restrictions, but most students aren't competing in these, so why are they being confined to certain sports? Some schools offer a wider range of activities, but these, too, are often highly gendered and tend to be kept to GCSE classes. Many arguments for segregated classes play into social stereotypes about gender, not least that girls might be embarrassed or uncomfortable playing alongside boys. Yet it can be argued that "a controlled environment is actually the best opportunity for pupils to learn how to respect each other".[144]

Surveys have explored girls' attitudes to PE. The Youth Sport Trust has reported that girls prefer less competitive PE lessons and that satisfaction with their body image declines rapidly around the age of 13.[145] A Girlguiding report[146] found that 43% feared being judged over their appearance and 24% felt that harassment and intimidation from boys might stop them taking part. Those statistics are simply unacceptable: we wouldn't accept sexual harassment in a classroom with desks and chairs, so why would we accept it in a PE class? We also don't accept the excuse of lack of confidence in other lessons – we work with students to boost their abilities and their self-assurance. It's clear that more work needs to be done. We are battling against a tsunami of social media messages and social judgement about appearance, but these are increasingly targeted at boys, too. PE is a great opportunity for students to develop positive and healthy relationships with their own bodies.

144. John Dabell, "The gender gap in PE", eteach.com, 30 November 2017

145. *Key Findings From Girls Active Survey,* Youth Sport Trust, November 2017

146. *Girls' Attitudes Survey 2017,* Girlguiding

Changing attitudes

Studies are divided on whether girls see sport as being "for boys" or not.[147] But many researchers agree that girls' barriers are formed by their perceived lack of ability and negative experiences, including PE teachers focusing on the "sporty ones". This belief that they aren't "good" at PE can lead to embarrassment and the impact on confidence and enjoyment is considerable. But we could reward achievement in ways other than simply winning: scoring, enabling a goal, regular participation and consistent effort are all important motivators when it comes to PE and activity. What *are* our goals for school PE? Do we want to create winning athletes, or a generation of adults who love to move and have healthy relationships with their bodies? I'd say the latter is what our society most needs, particularly for women.

We also need to contend with deeply embedded traditional thinking about which sports are suitable for girls: they are more likely to receive positive social messages about participating in yoga and dance than in American football. But gendered PE isn't the only way to go and many schools successfully embrace mixed classes. Alleyn's School in south-east London has a mixed cricket team – the head of lower school, Stuart Turner, has said that "the most successful girls are actually the fastest bowlers as well, so they are on a physical footing with the boys".[148] Having mixed-sex teams at all levels reminds spectators and supporters that equality is important.

This can be difficult in adolescence, when girls and boys may well be more conscious of their bodies, but they will be self-conscious whether they're in a single-sex group or a mixed one. Instead of segregating students, every effort should be made to build their body confidence. Allowing students to dress comfortably for physical activity and wear their own kit, for example, can make a big difference.

147. Abigail R Wetton, Rebecca Radley, Angela R Jones and Mark S Pearce, "What are the barriers which discouraged 15-16 year-old girls from participating in team sports and how can we overcome them?", *BioMed Research International*, 2013

148. Charlotte Phillips, "Mixed-team sports: why gender doesn't matter", *Independent School Parent*, 2017

Opportunities to develop sports leadership skills can build students' confidence and self-esteem, as well as their sporting ability and participation[149] – girls can take on roles such as sports leaders, internal ambassadors and lesson coaches. Their personal targets should be positive and healthy, focusing on themselves and their own development, and these should be core components of their assessment. It should be OK to sometimes remove competition and comparison from the equation in core PE.

Promoting the benefits

Girls need strong role models in sport. We all lack body confidence at times, but when we treat our bodies kindly and explore their strength, it does wonders for our physical and mental fitness. Incorporating role models into whole-school displays, assemblies and events, even training sessions, can help girls to picture themselves in similar positions and normalise girls in sport. The campaign This Girl Can is fantastic for resources and ideas to enthuse girls about sport. Its images deliberately feature a wide range of body types, alongside statements emphasising that exercise is hard but rewarding. Jessica Ennis-Hill, Kelly Holmes, Tanni Grey-Thompson and Simone Biles are great sporting role models who have all spoken candidly about what they find difficult and how they overcome it.

Active girls are more likely to have active mothers and friends; they are less influenced by what their friends do and less likely to agree that getting sweaty is unfeminine. We need to tackle the ubiquitous idea that femininity goes hand in hand with the ideal hair and makeup – both of which go out the window after a good exercise session.[150] It's difficult to break down the barriers of self-confidence surrounding being on display. Our efforts need to go beyond the sports hall and into the way that girls' appearances are discussed and explored across the curriculum, to help them build the body confidence they need.

149. *Girls Active 2017-2019*, Youth Sport Trust, 2019
150. *Changing the Game, for Girls*, Women's Sport and Fitness Foundation, 2012

Emphasising the mental fitness benefits of sport can improve participation and effort among girls. A study by Dr Katherine Appleton found that even over a two-week period – too short a time to have contributed to physical change – exercise improved participants' opinions of their bodies.[151] Although a small study, this should have an impact on what we discuss with girls to boost their participation. It's especially important to emphasise that at stressful times, like revision season, finding the time for exercise or making more effort in PE can really pay off. Studies show that efficacy in exams is heightened if physical activity is maintained.[152]

The kinds of sporting activity on offer should be considered, too. Although the traditional three-a-year model might have disappeared from some schools, it's still the preferred curriculum structure in many. We need to provide a range of activities, for girls and boys. Do students have access to activities that develop all areas of the body? Activities that help them to focus on their bodies, and pay attention to how sport feels and what it does in a positive way? A long-term goal of the PE curriculum should surely be – like any other subject – to foster a love of the subject that can transform their adult lives. Are there opportunities for students to take risks and be creative? Playing fun games is a way to recapture the joyful spirit of the primary playground. "Rabble" classes take place in local parks and community centres around the UK and are inspired by childhood games like British Bulldog and Capture the Flag.[153]

The Daily Mile initiative is popular in many primary schools[154] – it aims to get children to walk, jog or run an extra mile a day. Unsurprisingly, those who did so were significantly healthier, with better fitness and body composition than those who didn't. Placing route signs

---

151. "Short-term exercise boosts body image without making any physical difference", *British Psychological Society Research Digest*, 7 February 2013

152. Celia Álvarez-Bueno, Caterina Pesce, Iván Cavero-Redondo, Mairena Sánchez-López, Miriam Garrido-Miguel, Vicente Martínez-Vizcaíno, "Academic achievement and physical activity: a meta-analysis", *Pediatrics*, 140:6, November 2017

153. joinrabble.com

154. thedailymile.co.uk

around school, encouraging tutor groups to take part and organising lunchtime "walk and talk" sessions can help students to enjoy being more active – and build good habits for the future.

AUDIT QUESTIONS

- What resources in the school and local community (human, equipment and facilities) are being used to model, support and encourage regular activity for all students?
- Do teachers model active lifestyles or discuss their sporting achievements with students?
- Are newsletters, displays, posters, websites, blogs, social media platforms, assemblies and tutor group activities used to honour active women and girls from the school and community?
- Does the school celebrate a wide range of physical activities, e.g. taking part in charity walks/runs, leadership students engaging younger children in fun activities, or mothers and daughters participating in activities together?
- In a gender audit, what are the differences between boys and girls in terms of active participation in PE lessons, use of the full range of facilities and club attendance?
- Are sports clubs social as well as competitive?
- Are students encouraged to participate no matter their ability level and is their effort recognised?
- Is a range of activities available across year groups?
- Are PE classes mixed or segregated? When was this last reviewed and is it still a valid decision?

FURTHER RESOURCES

The Daily Mile provides a range of resources and trackers to encourage school-wide participation in walking or running for 15 minutes every day. *thedailymile.co.uk*

School Games provides a framework for school sporting competitions, leading to county and national finals. *yourschoolgames.com*

Sportsafe maintains a list of grant-giving organisations that can help to fund sporting development. *sportsafeuk.com/corporate-social-responsibility/grants-for-schools*

Sports Leaders is a programme offering qualifications in dance and sport leadership. Students learn to deliver activity sessions and clubs, building their own confidence and ability. *sportsleaders.org*

This Girl Can is a campaign celebrating female exercise, strength and movement in any form. Its website offers creative and imaginative ideas, and has a very supportive community. *thisgirlcan.co.uk*

The Youth Sport Trust promotes sport and activity for children. It runs National School Sport Week, as well as providing CPD and training for staff and students (including the Girls Go Gold programme). *youthsporttrust.org*

9. The arts

The main thing is to be moved, to love, to
hope, to tremble, to live – Auguste Rodin

As I wrote in the introduction, one of the most important aspects of
a feminist education is the explicit appreciation of those traditionally
feminine values: compassion, empathy, collaboration, listening,
nurturing. The arts are an ideal place to foster that appreciation, because
creativity is ultimately about a conversation – with the deeper parts of
ourselves and with the society we live in.

The arts are at risk of becoming marginalised in British education,
particularly with the introduction of the EBacc, which doesn't include
subjects like art and design, dance, design and technology, drama, music
and so on. These subjects do, however, contribute to a school's Progress
8 score. The 2019 Ofsted framework includes the following requirements
for its curriculum intent:

> "The school's curriculum is rooted in the solid consensus
> of the school's leaders about the knowledge and skills that
> pupils need in order to take advantage of opportunities,
> responsibilities and experiences of later life. In this way,
> it can powerfully address social disadvantage ... There

is high academic/vocational/technical ambition for all pupils, and the school does not offer disadvantaged pupils or pupils with SEND a reduced curriculum."[155]

Entrance figures for arts qualifications reflect a decline of 38% at GCSE between 2010 and 2019 (against a fall of 6.2% in the size of the Year 11 cohort) and a drop of 29% in A-level entries over the same period.[156] (The A-level decline seems to have been exacerbated by the removal of AS levels, which has prompted many schools to reduce their A-level offering.) Disadvantaged students, who are often less able to access the arts at home, are being disproportionately affected. The decline is accompanied by a similar fall in BTEC vocational qualifications[157] and a significant recruitment drive for STEM subjects.

Funding and timetabling are no doubt playing a major part – arts subjects are resource- and budget-heavy when done well. Fewer teachers are qualifying in these areas, too, so the subjects are often taught by non-specialists on timetables that use carousels, which can mean that the knowledge and experience available to students are limited.[158] Even from a purely economic perspective, this is madness. The arts contribute £10.8 billion to the UK economy and approximately 364,000 jobs. Productivity in the arts is higher than in the economy as a whole, with an estimate of £62,000 per worker compared with £46,800 per worker overall.[159]

Arts careers remain incredibly attractive for knowledgeable, creative individuals. And, as a report for the Higher Education Policy Institute has suggested, the industry is less susceptible to future automation or

---

155. *School Inspection Handbook,* Ofsted, November 2019

156. "Further drop in arts GCSE and A level entries for 2019", Cultural Learning Alliance, 22 August 2019

157. "GCSE results: further decline in arts and technical subjects", *The Conversation,* 21 August 2019

158. Professor John Last, *A Crisis in the Creative Arts in the UK?,* Higher Education Policy Institute, September 2017

159. *Contribution of the Arts and Culture Industry to the UK Economy,* Arts Council England, April 2019

dramatic change involving removal of roles, making it an attractive long-term prospect. The report concludes:

> *"Our great tradition in the creative industries is not because our nation is somehow innately creative. Rather, it is because we have created a strong arts education system through primary and secondary schools to further and higher education. As other countries seek to emulate this 'pipeline' we are in danger of fracturing it ... You do not enrich the nation's cultural and social life by starving it of talent, nor is that the best way to feed the economy."*[160]

It feels as though the focus has shifted towards skills and away from knowledge, when surely the ideal is a balance between the two. Creativity is far stronger when it is underpinned by knowledge and an understanding of oneself as an artist in communication with the past. All artists (in whatever field) build on or react to what has gone before; by educating our students in that rich tradition, we not only develop their cultural capital, but also give them the ability to contribute to that social conversation. When 60% of creative jobs are taken by graduates, compared with 30% of all jobs in the UK, we shouldn't focus on skills in isolation, but also build the knowledge to drive those skills forward.

Heart of the curriculum

The arts are the emotional core of the curriculum, where students are asked to express themselves and their identities – an intrinsic part of their development. Arts subjects celebrate multiple perspectives and enable young people to establish qualitative relationships based on their own values and experiences.[161] Taking on different roles and listening to alternative perspectives can develop empathy in students.

---

160. Professor John Last, *A Crisis in the Creative Arts in the UK?*, Higher Education Policy Institute, September 2017

161. Elliot W Eisner, "What can education learn from the arts about the practice of education?", *Journal of Curriculum and Supervision*, 18:1, 2002

Subjects that encourage physical self-expression, such as drama or dance, are so important for promoting a healthy, nurturing relationship with the body. They are an opportunity for students to use their bodies positively, as expressive tools, and they press pause on the self-criticism generated by the visually driven world of social media.

Banishing perfectionism

For girls in particular, arts subjects are a chance to address their perfectionist tendencies – the arts require experimentation, re-evaluation and reworking. Rather than describing work as "finished", it can be useful to refer to "stopping work on it" instead. With creative endeavours, a point can be reached – hopefully – where the piece has helped us to refine our skills and we'd like to start all over again. The best thing to do is to take those improved skills and knowledge and move on to a new piece of work. Nothing can ever be perfect, but it can part of a process.

Producing more work can also help to beat perfectionism. In their book *Art and Fear,* David Bayles and Ted Orland describe a ceramics class split in two. Half the class had to produce one perfect pot; the other half were to be graded by the weight of what they produced. By the end of the semester, those who had made more work were producing pots of higher quality.[162] Bear in mind that repetitive practice has to take place alongside some self-reflection and deliberate thought: students mustn't just churn out poor copies of one thing over and over again. But enabling them to produce as much as possible is an effective way to unlock the creative power that is sometimes stifled by perfectionism and lack of practice.

Access to the arts also supports students' mental and emotional development and their wellbeing. It reduces anxiousness, lowers production of the stress hormone cortisol, lessens stress symptoms, enables people to enter "flow" states where they focus on themselves, and can strengthen emotional resilience. Then there are the physical benefits of subjects like dance and drama, or the fine motor skills developed in art and music.[163]

162. David Bayles and Ted Orland, *Art and Fear: observations on the perils (and rewards) of artmaking,* Image Continuum Press, 2001
163. *Arts, Health and Well-being,* Welsh NHS Confederation, May 2018

Exploring gender bias

The gender bias attached to many arts subjects means boys often see them as a waste of time – too difficult for the time investment needed or too restrictive.[164] To address this we need to encourage discussion of the value of creative arts in the workplace, as well as reiterating the broader purposes of education and the advantages that students can gain from them.

Whereas boys tend to take arts subjects if they feel they'll benefit from them career-wise, girls' motivations appear to be more intrinsic and focused on enjoyment of the subject for its own sake.[165] Breaking down these masculine barriers is necessary to balance recognition of the arts and ensure that the subjects aren't marginalised along with the girls studying them.

Extracurricular opportunities can enrich students' everyday experiences of art. The Arts Award – at bronze, silver and gold level – enhances students' creative skills and knowledge, their understanding of the industry and their ability to teach others the skills they have learned.[166] Project qualifications (higher and extended) are also great ways for students to pursue creative ideas. Although EPQs often focus on the essay product as preparation for university, there is a brilliant production option in which students can create an artefact:

> *"An artefact can be a physical outcome such as a book or a short film or it can be a presentation to a specific audience, a play, it could be an event such as a fashion show or a musical evening. In fact there is almost no limit to what can constitute an artefact, as long as it has research at its core."*[167]

---

164. Margaret A Etherington, *How Girls' Achievements in School Art are Undermined by Boys' Rejection of the Subject*, presented at the British Educational Research Association Annual Conference, September 2008

165. Ibid.

166. artsaward.org.uk

167. *Quick Guide to Artefacts*, AQA, accessed 2019

This is an interesting option for those students wary of taking a creative GCSE and worried that a lack of expertise will prevent them from getting a good grade. These projects are about experimentation, exploration, preparation and planning, rather than a completely accomplished outcome.

Gender bias still exists in the creative industries, although it varies widely by the type of industry and there are plenty of movements working to improve the situation. A good careers programme is vital in schools, one that gives students the chance to meet practising artists from all disciplines. You could run enrichment projects in which current artists explore their own art with students, as well as the practicalities of making a living from art. For example, I attended a workshop run by Adrian Wood, who has a degree in fine art sculpture and is now a professional blacksmith; he makes beautiful work and runs weekend courses teaching people on portable forges.[168] Local places that deliver workshops and training can be an interesting source of speakers – they're often very happy to come in to school and chat to students about making a living from their art.

You could also invite other practitioners who *aren't* making a living from their art, but love doing it anyway. Local craft fairs are often a great source of people – there are so many amazing artistic crafters who pursue their work alongside another job and are really happy doing so. Local amateur theatre companies have actors, directors and stage crew who adore the creative outlet their hobby provides; they can help to communicate to students that value isn't just measured in earning capacity. Education is about lifelong learning and experiences.

Practical strategies

In the arts, perhaps more than other subjects, students benefit from seeing their own teachers as practitioners. Of course, not every teacher of art will be an expert in every discipline (and this can be explored in a discussion of expertise and specialism), but it's important that teachers share their own experiences and practise wherever possible.

---

168. awartistblacksmiths.co.uk

Broaden students' understanding of these creative subjects and allow them (where possible) to experiment with their own creativity. In art, for example, if students are interested in computer animation or knitting, allow scope for these areas to be explored alongside the more traditional forms. Extracurricular opportunities are great for encouraging students to experiment more freely with the arts; clubs can be successfully led by older students who share their own expertise.

Take opportunities to manage group work in relation to gender – for example, ensuring classes and small groups are gender-balanced. Drama teachers can use gender-blind casting and discuss the representation of gender in performance; other teachers can discuss gender balance in their fields.

Encourage playful approaches like messy art – playgroup-style sessions where students are able to experiment, use their hands to work with materials and simply have fun. They can remember what they used to enjoy about art as small children, before the perfectionism and expectation kicked in.

- Have we looked at the range of practitioners taught, checking for any gender bias, including by discipline?
- Do we explicitly discuss perfectionism with students, providing them with deliberate opportunities to make mistakes and start again?
- Do we refer to work as "finished", or make sure students know that the process involves moving on when the work has served its purpose?
- Do we take opportunities to explicitly demonstrate to students the qualitative skills they are developing: empathy, communication and collaboration?
- Have we explored gender gaps in arts subjects, including any disparity in take-up and achievement between girls and boys?
- Do students have the chance to experiment with assessments (e.g. timings and approaches) to reduce the pressure they feel?
- Are there opportunities for students to experience the arts in extracurricular activities that expand and develop the curricular offering?
- Do teachers present themselves as practitioners of their art and model the practice of art to their students?
- Are arts subjects viewed as academically challenging and rigorous?

================= **FURTHER RESOURCES** =================

The Arts Award is similar in style to the Duke of Edinburgh's Award, and is designed to promote student participation in arts and the artistic industries. *artsaward.org.uk*

Arts organisations often run educational outreach programmes and are willing to discuss supporting individual schools, particularly local ones or those with disadvantaged cohorts.

Local organisations, museums and arts companies are usually very willing to discuss the delivery of educational talks or workshops.

Local universities tend to offer educational outreach run by faculty teams, who can deliver talks or workshops at the university or in-school.

Subject organisations such as the **National Association for the Teaching of Drama**, **Music Mark** and **One Dance UK** can be very supportive in the development of curricula and expertise. *natd.eu, musicmark.org.uk, onedanceuk.org*

Part III
The whole girl

When you grow up as a girl, the world tells you the things that you are supposed to be: emotional, loving, beautiful, wanted. And then when you are those things, the world tells you they are inferior: illogical, weak, vain, empty – **Stevie Nicks**

Most of my female students have, at one time or another, expressed frustration over the expectations that society has of women. They call them unrealistic and unachievable. They very confidently discuss the ways in which these expectations are narrow and contradictory. But they still feel the pressure. They know they're being measured against impossible standards when it comes to their bodies; they know social media is everybody's highlight reel; they know the odds of "having it all" are stacked against them. But they still can't entirely reject these pressures. Instead, they feel frustrated and angry that the expectations persist even as they're being told to leave them behind.

In **Part III: The whole girl**, I look at ways to help students develop their independence and self-identity, so they feel confident to express their authentic selves, rather than trying to fit into a confining model. Young women have to be able to openly and explicitly challenge the expectations and ideals that oppress them. Some of the chapters consider how girls can deal with the challenges of being a teenager, particularly the aspects of their lives where being female has an influence. Some chapters look at ways to support girls' emotional wellbeing and emotional intelligence, so they can develop the self-confidence and self-love required to stand up for themselves in a world that often wants them to sit down – and then claim that was what they wanted to do all along. And some chapters explore parts of the curriculum that I think need to be reconsidered in an overtly feminist way, such as financial literacy and PSHE.

10. Sexist language and sexual harassment

Women who accuse men, particularly powerful men, of harassment are often confronted with the reality of the men's sense that they are more important than women, as a group – Anita Hill, *Speaking Truth to Power*

Who would have thought something that happened that long ago could have such power? – Alice Sebold, *Lucky*

Everyday classroom language sets the tone for students' attitude and culture. Even seemingly innocuous phrases used by the teacher to get attention or silence, or to address a group, can subtly reinforce the notion that men go first or are the dominant group.[169] More often, though, sexist language in the classroom is a lot more overt and a lot more damaging.

---

169. In teaching A-level language, I've had many discussions about whether addressing classes as "boys and girls" or "guys" demonstrates sexism or not. Try addressing a whole class as "ladies" or "gals" for a linguistic equivalent – it just doesn't work. One can make the argument that by broadening the usage of "guys" to include women, it simply reinforces male hegemony by erasing women

I've brought sexist language and sexual harassment together in one chapter because if sexist language is in regular use and goes unchallenged, it creates a culture in which sexual harassment can occur. I think it's quite likely that a lot of the time, a teacher hears the language but the harassment is hidden – it takes place outside the classroom, away from direct scrutiny. The culture created by inappropriate, sexually charged language can be emotionally distressing and make the school environment feel uncomfortable, even threatening.

Two-thirds of female sixth-formers and a third of male sixth-formers say they have witnessed the use of sexist language.[170] Although the evidence isn't clear on this point, that disparity is worth thinking about – is it perhaps because male students do not classify some of what they hear as sexist? It's also likely that girls hear more sexist language because it is more commonly directed at them. In secondary schools, 64% of teachers hear sexist language on a weekly basis, with 29% hearing it every day.[171] Even in primary schools, 17% of teachers have witnessed sexual harassment. It's likely that there's an awful lot more going on out of earshot.

In a study by the National Education Union and UK Feminista, girls reported hearing comments such as these:

- You throw like a girl.
- Pussy.
- Slut, sket, slag, whore, cunt, twat.
- Don't be such a girl.

Most of these emphasise sexual double standards, or the perceived weakness and inferiority of women. There are some male equivalents: "man up", "dick", "wanker" and other much more graphic euphemisms for genitalia. These, too, often aim to promote a hostile masculinity focused on sex. The balance is difficult to strike – we don't want to imply

---

170. *"It's Just Everywhere": a study on sexism in schools – and how we tackle it,* National Education Union and UK Feminista, 2017

171. Ibid.

that all boys are perpetrating sexual harassment (and that all victims are female) but there are statistical biases.

Girls are more likely to be targets of sexual harassment, with more than a third saying they've experienced some kind of sexual harassment at school, compared with 4% of boys. There's likely to be some male under-reporting of incidents, but the difference is striking. This is more than echoed in adult women's experiences. A UK government report on sexual harassment[172] makes for deeply disturbing reading: 85% of women aged 18–24 have received unwanted sexual attention in public places. Being grabbed, brushed against, rubbed up against or shouted at is an everyday occurrence for many women. Such harassment frequently begins when girls are in school uniform, with 90% of British women experiencing street harassment before the age of 17 and 10% aged 10 or younger.[173] Ask any secondary class and the girls will tell you their stories of being shouted and whistled at.

Even "just" being catcalled across the street can make women feel powerless and vulnerable. The Commons Women and Equalities Committee found that up to 90% of women's experiences were not reported, either because women felt it wasn't "enough" to report or because they felt nothing would, or could, be done about it. The sad fact is that for most incidents, the latter is probably true. Statistics on rape convictions alone suggest so, although the fact that upskirting was made a criminal offence in April 2019 indicates a shift in attitude. Yet street harassment is still so prevalent that it's all too easy to think: what's the point of reporting it?

The author Margaret Atwood has written that when she asked a male friend why men feel threatened by women, he answered, "They are afraid women will laugh at them." When she asked some female students why women feel threatened by men, they said, "They are afraid of being killed."[174] These fears don't interfere with women's day-to-day

---

172. *Sexual Harassment of Women and Girls in Public Places*, House of Commons Women and Equalities Committee, 23 October 2018

173. Beth A Livingston, *Hollaback! International Street Harassment Survey*, Hollaback! and Cornell University, 2015

174. Margaret Atwood, *Second Words: Selected Critical Prose*, House of Anansi, 1982

lives, for the most part, other than influencing where we walk, how much we drink, what we wear and whether we carry our keys between our fingers on the way home. These thoughts are indisputably a part of many women's lives and the threats are evidenced in the sexual banter that has somehow become the acceptable face of misogyny. Even if the men who use sexist language never commit any physical harassment, they're playing into a misogynist culture that legitimises it. By claiming it's "just a joke", the perpetrator places the onus on the target to simply not be offended or to fire something back. We need to challenge this, putting the focus back on the perpetrator to reconsider the language they use.

The word "rape" is regularly used out of context, almost dangerously normalised as a euphemism for beating someone in a competition or experiencing a serious disappointment in a test. If you hear it, stop the lesson. Stop the discussion and ask the student to repeat it. Explain that rape is a serious, violent, deeply traumatising attack on someone to assert the rapist's power and the victim's powerlessness. Explain that joking about it in a casual or careless way can be extremely hurtful *and* harmful.[175]

Slang for female genitals has become increasingly violent and grotesque. Many terms either focus on blood and destruction or view the vagina as solely for male entertainment. When we hear these words, too, we must challenge them. Calling a vagina something inherently violent represents sex as a one-sided assault, rather recognising it as an act of two-way intimacy that involves pleasure for both individuals. It normalises violence against women.

Making reports of sexual harassment is one of our responsibilities under statutory safeguarding guidance. School safeguarding leads will log the details and contact the police as appropriate, but it's essential that all teachers are aware of the scale and scope of what constitutes sexual harassment, particularly with the numbers of incidents being reported by students. All young people should be encouraged to report what they experience, rather than putting up with it as "just part of life". Under the relationships and sex education guidance coming into force in

---

175. Matt Pinkett and Mark Roberts offer excellent practical advice on tackling these conversations in their book *Boys Don't Try?* (Routledge, 2019)

September 2020, students need to be taught what constitutes harassment. Lessons should also include discussion of how to respond. It's a pretty typical response to freeze, for example, and many victims of all levels of harassment feel regret about that later. But calling out someone who is catcalling or whistling can put students in a dangerous position. We need to discuss how and when to challenge a perpetrator directly, as well as how and when to report them, and what kind of evidence (such as screenshots or photos) is useful to keep.[176]

Explore scenarios: when is it appropriate to speak to the harasser? When is it better to involve a friend, colleague or teacher? Literally script responses – although students aren't likely to remember them exactly in the moment, discussing them gives them some tools to be able to formulate their own when it counts.

Identifying sexist language and harassment

Guidance from the Department for Education identifies the most common forms of sexist language and sexual harassment:[177]

- Telling sexual stories, making lewd comments, making sexual remarks about clothes and appearance, or calling someone sexualised names.
- Sexual "jokes" or taunting.
- Physical behaviour such as deliberately brushing against someone, interfering with someone's clothes, or displaying pictures, photos or drawings of a sexual nature.
- Non-consensual sharing of sexual images and videos.
- Sexualised online bullying.
- Unwanted sexual comments and messages, including on social media.
- Sexual exploitation, coercion and threats.

---

176. Be careful not to give the impression that evidence-gathering responsibility lies with the victim, which could deter them from reporting

177. *Sexual Violence and Sexual Harassment Between Children in Schools and Colleges*, Department for Education, May 2018

Upskirting, now illegal in the UK, is defined as taking pictures under someone's clothes without their knowledge, with the intention of viewing their genitals or buttocks, with or without underwear. Connected behaviour such as snapping bra straps or flipping up a girl's skirt should also be viewed as sexual harassment.

How to challenge sexist language

The intention is to get students to understand that the language they're using is unacceptable. They need to be aware that it has the potential to harm others and that it reflects an inequality that needs to change. We can take several approaches to challenging such behaviour:

Organisational	• The school doesn't tolerate sexist language like that. • We're all responsible for making school a safe place to be. Language like that makes people feel unsafe because of its sexism.
Questioning	• What makes you think that? • What do you mean by that? • Let's talk about why people think like that. • How do you think that comment will make the people around you feel?
Confronting	• Language like that is not acceptable. • A lot of people would find that offensive. • Sexist language is as insulting as racist or homophobic language.
Personal	• I'm not happy with what you said. • I find that language really offensive. • I don't agree with that, because…

Preventative strategies are always better. Discussing sexist language with students is a way to encourage them to think more carefully about their choices. When they hear this language all around them, it's essential that in schools we deliberately identify the problems with it.

In a lesson, for example, ask students to list all the insults they have heard for men and women. Then ask them to categorise them in various ways. There will usually be a pretty quick and clear link with sexualised behaviour or genitalia, which can be used to begin exploring why the language itself is problematic.

Everyday sexist language

Although the language associated with harassment is the easiest to spot, other types of sexist language can also perpetuate gender stereotypes. Consider the examples that we use. Do we always present men as stronger, emotionally or physically, and position women as victims or less powerful in some way? Even drawing attention to gender might actually reinforce the negative stereotypes. If, for example, every time we mention a female scientist we add that this woman was overlooked for some award or denied recognition for a discovery, the message becomes that women don't get their due respect and consideration in the sciences.

Clothing and dress codes

In her book *Everyday Sexism*, Laura Bates addresses the victim-blaming that continues to surround school dress codes (primarily in the US, but also in many colleges and sixth forms in the UK). She describes girls being reprimanded or excluded for wearing spaghetti straps or leggings, or for revealing their shoulders. These were against the school dress code, but why?

Dress codes are a tricky thing and they provoke a lot of discussion – ultimately, they have to be designed for each individual school. We should interrogate our dress codes once in a while and make sure that our decisions remain valid. If the restrictions are aimed more at minimising "boys' distraction" then we're sending dangerous messages to both genders about what is and isn't acceptable.

Is it OK to have separate dress codes for girls and boys? Do we have to mandate that boys all wear a suit, for example? Or is "smart business dress" an appropriate guideline for all? We might, then, give some examples of what that means. The Government Equalities Office advice is primarily aimed at preventing dress codes that overly sexualise women – those that require them to wear high heels or make-up. But it also includes this:

"Any requirement to wear make-up, have manicured nails, wear hair in certain styles or to wear specific types of hosiery or skirts is likely to be unlawful, assuming there is no equivalent requirement for men."[178]

For many schools, setting a required skirt length could fit into this category. Although it's lawful to insist on a "smart" dress code, gender-specific requirements are not lawful. Skirt length is often a source of conflict with young women, and it seems that objections are frequently made because they're too short and revealing. How much of this comes from a deep-seated belief that women should be "covered up" more? There is a line, sometimes literally, between being able to see someone's underwear when they go upstairs and thinking that their skirt is too short without being able to articulate why. The first example might lead to a conversation about personal safeguarding responsibilities (if upskirting is a crime, then being able to see up someone's skirt accidentally probably isn't helpful), but the second is more a matter of social expectation. Being truly feminist means interrogating these ideas and trying to decide where our opinions come from. If they come from a position of gender bias, let's rethink them. This doesn't mean we can't distinguish between professional and informal modes of dress, but let's have some good reasons for doing so.

---

178. *Dress Codes and Sex Discrimination: what you need to know*, Government Equalities Office, May 2018

- Do we address sexist language and sexual harassment directly in school policies?
- Are staff and students aware of the definitions of sexual harassment and its various forms?
- Do we discuss ways in which students can guard against harassment, and measures they can take to report and stop it?
- Are all incidents of harassment reported and recorded by staff?
- Is the use of sexist language reported and recorded in the same way as other discriminatory language (e.g. homophobic or racist)?
- Are there opportunities for students to discuss sexist language and its impact on social culture?
- Are staff conscious of the examples they choose and how these can perpetuate gender stereotypes?
- Are students challenged in their use of sexist language and made aware of its impact on others?
- Have we recently reviewed our dress code in terms of gender bias?

FURTHER RESOURCES

Hollaback! provides resources on rights and awareness, guides for teachers and information on how to fight back against harassment. *ihollaback.org*

I Have The Right To, a website founded by Chessy Prout, a survivor of high-school sexual assault, includes resources, interviews and advice. *ihavetherightto.org*

Memoirs by sexual assault and harassment survivors include **Lucky** by Alice Sebold, **Girl in the Woods** by Aspen Matis and **Speaking Truth to Power** by Anita Hill.

Maybe He Just Likes You by Barbara Dee is a novel about a 12-year-old girl experiencing harassment at school.

Rape Crisis, **Safeline** and **Safeline Young People** offer online resources, and provide online and telephone counselling to victims of sexual assault and those who are supporting them. Safeline also provides courses for education professionals and students. *rapecrisis.org.uk, safeline.org.uk, slyp.org.uk*

11. Healthy emotions

I hate to hear you talk about all women as if they were fine ladies instead of rational creatures. None of us want to be in calm waters all our lives – Jane Austen, *Persuasion*

Being a teenager is intensely emotional and it can be a full-time task just to understand your emotions, never mind trying to manage and accept them. Shifting relationships, exam pressure and hormones are a nightmare cocktail, especially when aggravated by a near-crippling need to sleep. Women and emotions are a tricky business. On the one hand, women are renowned for being emotional and emotionally expressive.[179] The words "empathetic", "communicative" and "intuitive" might be used to describe them, and there is a widespread belief that women express or experience a wider range of emotions.[180] On the other hand, more negative language is also associated with women and emotions: "whingy", "hysterical", "neurotic", "irrational", "dramatic". These words all imply that women are complaining about something trivial but doing it pretty vocally.

179. E Ashby Plant, Janet Shibley Hyde, Dacher Keltner and Patricia G Devine, "The gender stereotyping of emotions", *Psychology of Women Quarterly*, 24:1, 2000
180. Agneta H Fischer, "Sex differences in emotionality: fact or stereotype?", *Feminism and Psychology*, 3:3, 1993

One of my favourite pieces of angry-etymology (my students usually hear it in a heated debate about the need to interrogate language for hidden misogyny) is that the word "hysteria" comes from the Greek *hystera*, meaning womb.[181] Ancient Greek medical writers suggested that the womb moving through the body frequently caused physical and mental ill health.[182] The word connects the physical condition of being a woman with an *inappropriate* display of emotion – and here again we come up hard against social conditioning. Who decides what is or isn't appropriate? There are many emotions that women and girls are told they shouldn't express at all, like anger. Michelle Obama has spoken about having to moderate her speaking style: "I thought I was doing great telling my story, sharing it honestly. But my whole persona was distorted. This was the time I was called an angry black woman."[183] Even if women *are* angry, the accusation itself is often used as a way to dismiss their feelings and what they have to say. Too often, women are criticised for being *over*emotional and failing to walk the tightrope of appropriately demonstrated emotions.

Both genders suffer in this situation. The same studies that find we expect women to show a wide range of emotions suggest that men are expected to express limited and negative emotions like anger.[184] Men are more often socially conditioned to show their anger in physical violence (or sometimes a healthier physical release like competitive sport), while girls are told they can't express it at all (this is one explanation for girls' self-harming, as they seek to find a way to release intense emotions).[185] Men are told that they shouldn't express a full range of

---

181. etymonline.com

182. Jane Rowlandson, *Women and Society in Greek and Roman Egypt*, Cambridge University Press, 1998

183. Jessica Kegu, "Michelle Obama expected 'brilliance' when she got to Princeton – she was underwhelmed", CBS News, 14 November 2018

184. Ursula Hess, Sacha Senécal, Gilles Kirouac, Pedro Herrera, Pierre Philippot and Robert E Kleck, "Emotional expressivity in men and women: stereotypes and self-perceptions", *Cognition and Emotion*, 14:5, 2000

185. Patricia A Adler, *The Tender Cut: inside the hidden world of self-injury*, New York University Press, 2011

tender emotions,[186] while girls are made to feel abnormal if they don't feel an intense clenching of their ovaries when they see a picture of a baby. But, of course, girls *do* feel the more negative emotions like guilt, shame and embarrassment, and these can be seen from young adulthood.[187] It's the T-shirt syndrome I discussed in the introduction: be happy, smile and love others – don't admit to feeling anything else.

It's not OK for our society to police emotion in this way. And, in fact, our continuing repression of it is causing intense harm to young people, by teaching them to ignore how they feel. Our emotions can give us great joy and pleasure, but they also tell us when something isn't right – anger, misery and sadness can be signs that change is needed. Intuition comes from unconsciously processed information, which is often delivered to us in feelings: this doesn't feel quite right; that feels good. It's important to listen to our intuition, and repeatedly shutting down or ignoring our feelings can be unhealthy and lead us into danger.[188] It's very difficult to spot from the outside, but girls who aren't addressing their feelings are likely to exhibit behaviours such as:

- Looking after everyone else.
- Making a joke of everything.
- Almost obsessively planning, needing strict controls over their tasks and time.
- Physical behaviours like constant fidgeting, tapping or jiggling their legs.

All students, female and male, should be taught that their emotions matter – and they need to explore healthy ways to feel and show them. Fighting is not a healthy or productive expression of anger. But anger can

186. Matt Pinkett and Mark Roberts, *Boys Don't Try? Rethinking masculinity in schools,* Routledge, 2019

187. Tara Chaplin and Amelia Aldao, "Gender differences in emotion expression in children: a meta-analytic review", *Psychological Bulletin,* 139:4, 2012

188. Galang Lufityanto, Chris Donkin and Joel Pearson, "Measuring intuition: nonconscious emotional information boosts decision accuracy and confidence", *Psychological Science,* 27:5, 2016

be put to good use through protesting against injustice and making an argument for change, for example. By learning different ways to express emotions – right down to body language and ways of talking – students gain options when it comes to their emotional life and are reassured that everyone feels everything at some time in their life.

The language of mental ill health

We're more and more aware of the stigma surrounding mental health and illness, yet the language we use hasn't caught up. I've heard all of the following in my classroom:

- I'm a little bit OCD.
- Mental.
- Mad.
- Crazy.
- I have anxiety.
- I'm depressed.

Awareness is growing of the complexity of the language surrounding mental health and wellbeing, but there are plenty of terms that are increasingly generalised. I don't think adults would dream of saying, "I'm a bit anorexic today", but many are fine with saying, "I'm a little OCD". Obsessive-compulsive disorder has the potential to be very damaging to health, financial security and happiness – it's not about putting your fine liners in rainbow order. This is a flippant example, perhaps, but it's one I've heard a lot. Using language in this way can medicalise traits or preferences in a potentially dangerous way, not least because it makes students feel like what they're feeling isn't normal, when actually, it is. Everybody loves a rainbow. Lots of people like order and organisation. That's fine. Likewise, people feel sad, angry or a bit blue – it doesn't mean they're depressed. The full range of emotions is vital to human experience.

It's all very well saying it's OK to talk, but what are the actual messages that students are receiving? The positive psychologist Shawn Achor has an instructive example. On being asked to deliver a session at a "wellness week", he asked what the other sessions were covering. He was told they were about depression, eating disorders, bullying and school violence, illicit drugs and risky sex. That's not "wellness".[189] And it does matter. When we discuss mental ill health, do we deliver overwhelmingly negative messages? Do we always link to extreme examples of suicide and self-harm, or do we suggest ways in which students can improve their mental fitness, as they would their physical fitness? We must highlight that there is a difference between, for example, "I feel anxious" and "I have anxiety". The first is a feeling, and feelings are transitory – they can be experienced and they change. But "I have anxiety" begins to establish anxiety as a disorder that needs to be treated. Sometimes that is true. But we need to ensure that language is used carefully, so that it's possible to distinguish between students who need help and support to manage their everyday feelings (which can be intense!) and students who need something more.

We also need to remind students that these feelings are completely normal and appropriate. It's appropriate to feel a level of stress about exams or important occasions. It's appropriate to feel anger and grief when someone dies or a relationship ends. We shouldn't reject or repress those feelings because they're uncomfortable and unpleasant. Everyone needs to be able to feel them.

Soothe-drive-threat systems

There are three basic emotional regulation systems in the brain.[190] The soothe-drive-threat systems all feed into one another, triggered by events, thoughts and hormonal changes. For most people, when it comes to achievement at school and work, the optimal would be to operate between the soothe and drive systems.[191] We would feel ambition and purpose, seek to take risks to achieve what we want, and feel safe and

---

189. Shawn Achor, "The happy secret to better work" (talk), ted.com, 2011
190. *Worksheet 5.3: threat/drive/soothe system*, Cumbria Partnership NHS Foundation Trust, accessed 2019
191. For a fuller explanation and a great discussion of the soothe-drive-threat systems in education, read Andy Sammons' *The Compassionate Teacher* (John Catt, 2019)

trusted enough to do so. In lessons, this is the ideal situation: students are challenged, want to work hard and feel supported to give it a go. The threat system isn't activated because they know they will be learning even if they find the work hard or make mistakes. When the soothe and drive systems are operating, we enter what the psychologist Mihaly Csikszentmihalyi calls "flow",[192] that brilliant moment when students lose track of time and everything's just *working*; then they hear the bell and think, "That went fast!"

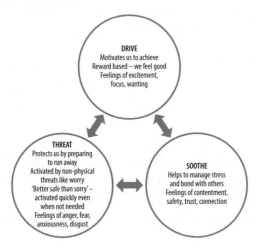

How resilient can one girl be?

The threat system has its uses: it alerts us to actual dangers, like speeding cars, physical violence or a terrible situation. But it's easily pushed into overdrive by the modern education system.

For example, I would argue that we've *made* exam preparation into a terrible situation for many students. They are given target grades based on data averages, and if they don't meet them then they're summoned to "interventions", have to endure difficult conversations and feel that they're being blamed for failure. Alongside this, they "know" that if they don't get the grades, they won't get the next training place or degree – so

---

192. Mihaly Csikszentmihalyi, *Flow: the psychology of optimal experience*, Rider, 1990

no job, no home, no family, no life. This might sound overdramatic, but this is the message society seems to present: failure on this day is the end of your future as you've planned it. Why *wouldn't* that send the threat system into overdrive?

As the media frequently reports, this pressure increasingly starts in primary schools, where 96% of headteachers say they are concerned about the impact of KS2 SATs on pupils' wellbeing.[193] Girls' lives can seem overwhelmingly threatening from all angles. A Girlguiding survey found that girls aged 11–16 were put off being leaders because:

- Female leaders are criticised more than male leaders (50%).
- They don't have enough confidence (46%).
- There's too much focus on their looks, not what they do (41%).
- Women are harassed for speaking out (32%).
- It's harder for women to make mistakes/take risks (32%).[194]

Those responses incorporate a whole host of issues: self-confidence; body image; the pressure of perfectionism; the belief that women are harassed, bullied and silenced. When you feel under threat simply for speaking your mind, it's no wonder the soothe-drive systems fail to function.

There's always going to be an element of conflict here. Some threat is good. It can (temporarily) boost performance, which is very useful in examination or competition situations. Adrenaline can provide a little burst of energy and focus to get students through difficult things. But we have to be conscious of designing a school system where the threat response is too regularly triggered, leading to anxiousness when the body is unable to relax and the soothe function can't work. We also need to teach students some practical ways to activate their soothe-drive systems. The most successful students can already do this to an extent; they are able not only to power through their exams, but even to enjoy them. Demonstrating our expertise to the best of our ability is a powerful

---

193. Helen Ward, "Sats create needless pressure for teachers and pupils, heads warn", *TES*, 19 March 2019
194. *Girls' Attitudes Survey 2019*, Girlguiding, 2019

and empowering act, but only if we're able to enjoy it because the threat system is well under control.

Harnessing the drive system

The drive system works best when goals are small and achievable and we celebrate our success. It works in a virtuous cycle: for most people, productivity is rewarding because it reinforces our view of ourselves as successful, active and purposeful. Success also empowers the drive system. Humans love doing well and getting praise – all the things that set off a little endorphin buzz in the brain. Success is literally addictive. In schools, we praise where praise is due, so we enable students to meet their smaller goals and then we celebrate their successes.

As teachers we set goals all the time, but not always explicitly with students. Our long-term and medium-term plans are ideal examples of goal-setting. We set a learning goal, break it down into tasks, schedule it and fulfil it. We adapt as we go, with the goal still in mind. Anyone who's done a Couch to 5k programme or similar will be familiar with this process: small, manageable and incremental steps; a very clear goal; success that is measurable (I can run 5k when I couldn't before!). Sharing this technique with students can help them to achieve their own successes.

SMART goals are often discussed as the best way to set goals. They are Specific, Measurable, Achievable, Realistic and Timely. This makes a lot of sense, especially the specific and measurable aspects – we only really get those affirmation endorphins if we knew what we were supposed to be achieving in the first place. Deadlines are tricky in education because assessment dates are often something students have no control over. Productivity experts talk about setting goals in pen and deadlines in pencil; if we make deadlines less high-stakes, then they become less threatening. Low-stakes testing, regular quizzing and so on aren't just good for long-term memory, but they also reduce the threat and tension surrounding assessment. The way we talk about assessments also helps to minimise this threat. *All* assessment until the external exam is formative; it's all designed to help us help students to improve and develop their skills. Talking about assessment in a productive and collaborative way diminishes the threat.

Neurolinguistic programming offers another framework for goal-setting: POWER.

P: outcomes are stated **positively**. "I want to be able to do exams in a clear and calm way" rather than "I want to get rid of exam stress".

O: the student's **own role** in making it happen. What do they have to do themselves (this might include enlisting support from others)?

W: **what specifically**? What is their starting point? What do they need to move on, including resources (time, physical, etc)?

E: what **evidence** will show their progress and success? Neurolinguistic programming also uses sensory evidence: what will they feel, hear and see? It can help students to mentally rehearse and visualise their outcome. A study by Trevor Day and Paul Tosey gives the example of preparing for an exam:

> *"Visual evidence might be the existence of a tidy desktop, annotations around their class notes, practice questions they had answered and had marked ... [Feelings and emotions] might be sensations of wellbeing and calmness, expressed in sensory specific terms. Such mental rehearsal can evoke sensory impressions that are more powerfully motivating than detached, abstract notions of 'what it takes to succeed' expressed in more conventional terms."*[195]

R: **relationships**, or what neurolinguistic programming calls an "ecology" check, about the different parts of a student's internal relationships and wellbeing. They need to see if the plan/decision "feels right" – and if it doesn't, they need to explore why. Factors might include demands on time (such as part-time work) or discomfort that could stem from expectations of themselves or others. Awareness of these barriers creates opportunities to solve these problems. "Intuition" is

195. Trevor Day and Paul Tosey, "Beyond SMART? A new framework for goal setting", *The Curriculum Journal*, 22:4, 2011

really responding to subconscious signals that we're hardly even aware of. Trying to be more mindful of our own intuitive responses and taking them seriously can help with confident decision-making.

Essentially, the SMART and POWER frameworks help to activate the drive system by making goals seem manageable, as well as providing a clear path towards them that minimises the threat system. Either way, students also need help to break down goals. It's no good setting them a target of seven grade 6s and expecting them to work it out – they need a series of manageable steps.

Self-help and goal-setting coaches also use visualisation, which is part of the soothe-drive system and can be really effective for many students. The E in POWER utilises this to some extent, asking students to visualise what they will think, feel and experience as a result of their success. Students can either imagine or write down their feelings (in the present tense – it's more powerful than the future tense)[196] or create a mood board to help them imagine the situation.

Learning to self-soothe

The soothe system is triggered by different things for different people, and different things at different times, too. If your go-to relaxing trigger is heavy rock music, there can still be moments when only Classic FM will do! Girls need time and strategies to figure out what works for them, but these are some areas to explore with them:

- **Noise.** Quiet or silence is ideal for deep work. But if the threat system or anxiousness are in control, a specific song or playlist can help to shift their mood.
- **Lighting.** Softer light from multiple sources is most soothing.
- **Warmth.** Hot-water bottles, warm drinks, heat packs and even standing by a radiator for a few minutes can all contribute to a feeling of comfort. Physical comfort can help adrenaline to subside.

---

196. Kathryn J Lively, "Affirmations: the why, what, how, and what if?", *Psychology Today*, 12 March 2014

- **Belly breathing**. This is a useful classroom technique because it's easy to do quietly and without being noticed by others. Breathing from the belly, feeling it moving up and down rather than the ribs or shoulders, can lead to deeper and more calming breaths. Ideally, belly breathing is accompanied by checking in with the body, stretching anywhere that feels tense or tight.
- **A "play" list** of 15–20 things that they find fun and joyful. These should be more or less free, relatively quick and easily accessible. Relaxation and rest strengthen us, so several of these things should be included each week when students are scheduling their time.

Some of these are difficult to implement in a classroom situation, but with a little creativity they can work consistently. Our education system can be inherently stressful for young people, not only because of the mental stresses of learning, but also because of the pace of modern life, the extrovert nature of many schools and the emotional intensity of teenagers' lives. As well as strategies for recuperation and strengthening the soothe-drive systems, students require a different narrative – one that offers them support and inspiration if they don't get the grades they want. This honours the intrinsic value of education and celebrates a full range of achievement beyond the academic.

Improving mental fitness

In his book *The Happiness Advantage*, Shawn Achor radically reverses the usual expectations of happiness and success.[197] Instead of finding that success brings happiness, his research actually proved the opposite. He found that happy people were more productive and more successful, with better creativity, memory and problem-solving abilities, because their soothe-drive systems were able to be in control. This kind of happiness acts as a sort of vaccination against stress by creating genuine resilience. There will always be stressful times, but if you start from a happier and

197. Shawn Achor, *The Happiness Advantage: the seven principles that fuel success and performance at work*, Virgin, 2011

more positive baseline, then you'll be better able to cope. Achor suggests five activities to boost happiness and resilience:

- **Cardio exercise**: 15 minutes at a time, three times a week.
- **Daily journaling**. Write a few sentences or bullet points about something positive that has happened to you.
- **Daily gratitude**. Every day, write down three things you are grateful for. They can be deep and profound, but they don't have to be! The fact that it was sunny, you caught the bus after leaving late and you really enjoyed your morning coffee are all worth focusing on.
- **Meditate**. There are apps such as Calm or Headspace, but it is just as effective to simply concentrate on slow belly breathing for a few minutes. Any posture is good, but lying flat on the floor in the shavasana yoga pose encourages relaxation through focus on the body.
- **Thanking/acts of kindness**. Send a thank-you card or do something nice for another person.

There are more strategies for mental fitness in chapter 14, but something all students can benefit from is time-tracking and management. Particularly for girls, who are very active but put a lot of pressure on themselves, this can be a way to slow down a little. For some, it can also provide the motivation to rearrange their time in order to meet their real goals:

- For two weeks, **keep a record** of everything that happens in half-hour blocks. *Everything*, including eating, sleeping and commuting.
- **Look at the balance**. Does it feel right? Is there a balance across the week? Are you getting eight hours' sleep? Some girls have found that rating their mood out of eight a few times a day can help to identify anxiousness triggers. A daily balance isn't necessary, but looking at the balance over a week or month can indicate where priorities can be shifted or extra time spent.

Even if students aren't struggling, they often benefit from time-tracking. Too often I have students telling me, usually late in Year 11 or 13, that they plan to do a huge amount of revision but not give up any activities or paid work. They literally, physically, don't have the time and put themselves under huge pressure. But seeing that on paper gives them power over their own actions. They can choose to revise or choose to work. I can't make them choose revision, but I can help them to make an informed decision.

Sometimes I ask students to plan their ideal day first, then compare it with reality. It's also worth making them aware that things change: at different times of year, their schedules can and should shift depending on what's most important.

When it comes to mental fitness, we need to remember the importance of recovery time. In physical fitness training, the body needs time after a workout to recover and repair. In mental fitness, the same is often true. Yet in an average school day, when every lesson needs to be "challenging" and breaks are spent comparing scores, Instagrams and weekend plans, where is the recovery time? I'm not suggesting a week of films after every mock season, but a proportional change of pace.

- Do students have opportunities to discuss emotions and the healthy/ unhealthy ways to express and harness those?
- Are students introduced to techniques to manage their emotions and self-soothe?
- Do students learn how to manage their time and expectations?
- Are students taught to activate their drive system through good goal-setting and review processes?
- Are students' achievements celebrated regularly, whatever they might be?
- Have we looked at our school calendar by year group to identify stressful periods? How can the stress be minimised?
- Is there proportional recovery time after these stressful periods (e.g. mock exams) or do students go straight back into challenging lessons?
- How can we prepare students to cope with times of stress?
- Do we celebrate a range of achievements (not just academic ones), including effort?

FURTHER RESOURCES

Kooth provides online, free and anonymous support for young people through moderated online communities. Experienced counsellors are available to chat. *kooth.com*

A Mighty Girl offers a book list entitled "Understanding the way I feel", with recommendations across the age ranges, including fiction and non-fiction, and workbooks to explore emotions. *amightygirl.com/blog?p=11449*

NHS Moodzone offers suggestions and audio guides (more suitable for older students) on how to address common mood problems. *nhs.uk/conditions/stress-anxiety-depression*

The Open University's "Succeed with learning" course is available to anyone for free. It includes modules on goal-setting, how to learn and wider perspectives on learning. *tinyurl.com/v9lxlhb*

YoungMinds is a charity that supports young people's mental wellbeing, with resources for students, parents and teachers. *youngminds.org.uk*

12. Relationships and sex education

We teach girls shame. Close your legs; cover yourself. We make them feel as though, being born female, they're already guilty of something. And so, girls grow up to be women who silence themselves. They grow up to be women who cannot say what they truly think. And they grow up – and this is the worst thing we do to girls – they grow up to be women who have turned pretence into an art form – **Chimamanda Ngozi Adichie**

I am done living in a world where women are lied to about their bodies; where women are objects of sexual desire but not subjects of sexual pleasure; where sex is used as a weapon against women; and where women believe their bodies are broken, simply because those bodies are not male. And I am done living in a world where women are trained from birth to treat their bodies as the enemy – **Emily Nagoski, *Come As You Are***

Sexuality might be the most overrated and underrated aspect of adult life. On the one hand, we are overwhelmed with suggestions that everyone (else) is having amazing sex all the time and that if you're not, there's something seriously wrong. On the other hand, the statistics paint a picture of increasing uncertainty and unhappiness about sex, sexual identity, pleasure and experience. And then there are the gender binaries that come into play: men as players, bachelors and studs who gain social status from sex; women who are sluts or frigid, and shamed for having sex too early, too late, too much or not enough. This binary serves neither boys nor girls and it isn't disappearing as fast as we might hope. A study published in the *British Medical Journal* found that sexual behaviour generated a lot of anxiousness, usually born out of dissatisfaction and comparisons with what was regarded as "normal", as well as perceptions of everyone else's experience.[198]

For both sexes, sex and knowledge of sex and sexuality is critical in developing self-confidence and self-esteem. Yet too many students leave school uneducated about sex and so they turn to ill-informed friends, the internet or pornography to find out about it.[199] Good relationships and sex education (RSE) is also a vital part of safeguarding: we have to teach girls – and boys – about sex and sexuality to help them look after themselves physically, mentally and emotionally. The UN sees comprehensive sex education as vital to meeting its 2030 sustainable development goals, because "quality education, good health and well-being, gender equality and human rights are intrinsically intertwined".[200]

This is a feminist issue where boys and girls can both benefit. Boys experience just as much mythology, pressure and stereotyping in this area as girls. They need to know it's perfectly normal to think about sex as often as they do, whether that's more or less than others. It's OK to be attracted to personalities more than appearance, and it's OK for them to decide for themselves the strength of their connections with sex, love, friendship, romance and desire. The #MeToo movement helped people to talk about sexual harassment, consent and entitlement, but the discussion never quite

198. Kaye Wellings, Melissa J Palmer, Kazuyo Machiyama and Emma Slaymaker, "Changes in, and factors associated with, frequency of sex in Britain: evidence from three National Surveys of Sexual Attitudes and Lifestyles (Natsal)", *British Medical Journal*, 2019

199. Peggy Orenstein, *Girls and Sex*, Harper, 2016

200. *International Technical Guidance on Sexuality Education: an evidence-informed approach*, UNESCO, 2018

moved beyond speaking up about unwanted sexual contact. Clearly, that's important and all students should know what to do in such situations. But RSE should also go beyond that, helping students to understand that although sex can be risky and lead to unintended consequences, it can also be pleasurable and fun, and part of an intimate and loving relationship, and have a lot of complicated factors related to physical and mental health attached to it. Current methods of teaching RSE risk reducing sex to a frightening experience, suggesting that that's the norm.

It might be a cliché but, as a nation, we're pretty poor at talking about sex in a way that is empowering and recognises that there is no such thing as "normal" when it comes to sexuality. Globally, the picture isn't too different. The International Planned Parenthood Federation notes that sex education worldwide focuses on the negative: disease, unwanted pregnancy, shame and self-loathing.[201] And student experiences of sex education are patchy: the IPPF found that 17% of male students rated it as "good" or "very good", compared with 11% of female students.

Statistics on how successful sex education is are tricky to analyse. But the third National Survey of Sexual Attitudes and Lifestyles (Natsal), conducted in the UK in 2010–12, found the following:

- 29% of women aged 16–24 had had sex with someone of the opposite sex before the age of 16.
- 16% of women aged 16–44 had had same-sex experience (up from 4% in 1990–91).
- The average number of opposite-sex partners for women aged 16–44 had increased from 3.7 (1990–91) to 7.7 (2010–12).
- Almost one in six people reported a health condition that had affected their sex life in the previous year, but less than one in four men and one in five women had sought help.
- 51% of women had experienced sexual difficulties in the previous year.

---

201. *Putting Sexuality Back Into Comprehensive Sexuality Education: making the case for a rights-based, sex-positive approach*, International Planned Parenthood Federation, August 2016

- One in 10 women and one in 71 men reported non-volitional sex (sex against their will) since the age of 13, and these people were more likely to report poorer physical and mental fitness.
- Of unplanned pregnancies among women aged 16–44 in the previous year, 21% were in women aged 16–19.[202]

It's clear that high-quality sex education is essential to help young women and men to explore, understand and appreciate an aspect of life that has traditionally been shrouded in duty, responsibility, risk, fear and shame.

What is a school's responsibility?
A few years ago, I probably would have said that RSE fell under parental responsibility, and that a school's role was to back up and support what parents were doing. I think differently about it now. A lot of parents experience similar shame and embarrassment, and have a really difficult time talking about sex with their children. If we want the next generation of parents to do things differently, then we need to get the current school generation talking about sex comfortably and confidently.

The statutory RSE guidance coming into force in September 2020 says it "must be taught sensitively and inclusively, with respect to the backgrounds and beliefs of pupils and parents while always with the aim of providing pupils with the knowledge they need of the law".[203] It says pupils should know:

- That they have a choice to delay sex or enjoy intimacy without sex.
- The facts around pregnancy, including miscarriage.
- The facts about the full range of contraceptive choices, efficacy and options.
- That all aspects of health (physical, emotional, mental, sexual and reproductive) can be affected by choices they make surrounding sex and relationships.

202. *Sexual Attitudes and Lifestyles in Britain: highlights from Natsal-3*, National Survey of Sexual Attitudes and Lifestyles 2010–12

203. *Relationships Education, Relationships and Sex Education (RSE) and Health Education*, Department for Education, 2019

- How and where to access confidential sexual and reproductive health advice and treatment.

There are a lot of positives here, but the *delivery* of RSE is critical. "Enjoy intimacy without sex" could become either a lesson on abstinence or an open discussion about consent, the variety of sexual activities and how to draw a line at a crucial moment.

What is good sex ed?

One of the principles of the IPPF declaration on sexual rights is that "sexuality, and pleasure deriving from it, is a central aspect of being human, whether or not a person chooses to reproduce".[204] The IPPF recommends that high-quality sex education should cover:

- **Sexuality.** Defined by the World Health Organization (WHO) as "a central aspect of being human throughout life [that] encompasses sex, gender identities and roles, sexual orientation, eroticism, pleasure, intimacy and reproduction".
- **Sexual health and wellbeing**, including the role played by sex in mental and emotional wellbeing. Sexual wellbeing is a major factor in safe and consensual sex, and has important repercussions in many aspects of adult lives.
- **Sexual rights**, including the right to express sexuality freely and without prejudice, as well as the right to be free from sexual coercion or control.
- **Sex positivity.** An attitude that celebrates sexuality as a part of life that brings happiness and energy. It aims to promote positive experiences, rather than solely preventing the negative. A sex-positive curriculum can tackle taboos and risks without reinforcing fear and shame.
- **Pleasure.** The WHO says sexual pleasure is a key component of sexual health – and, of course, it's often the primary motivation

204. *Sexual Rights: an IPPF declaration*, International Planned Parenthood Federation, 2008

for sex. The propensity of sex education to dwell on the negative risks reinforcing the idea that sexual power inequalities, abuse, disease, unwanted pregnancy and violation are the norm.[205]

Delivery of sex education

There's not a lot of research on whether mixed or single-sex classes are better in RSE, but there is evidence that girls and boys want to know they're being taught the same thing. Whether it's information about ejaculation or about periods, both sexes want the other to know it, too.

The curricular attitude to RSE often compounds the problems it faces. RSE is frequently delivered by non-specialists[206] and might well be taught in tutor time or in one-off "drop-down" sessions, which gives the impression that it's less important than the academic curriculum and puts the teaching staff at a significant disadvantage. Relationships with students are often very different in this kind of lesson, and it can be difficult to go back to teaching history or D&T to the students you taught RSE to the day before.

Teachers also bring their own backgrounds and experiences to sex education – they can be much harder to leave at the classroom door than our experiences of other subjects. Indeed, when we enter a classroom as an English teacher, we're encouraged to communicate our reading experiences, our love of the subject and our belief that it's the best thing ever. In a lesson focused on sex, however…! I certainly don't recommend abandoning professional boundaries, but we must recognise, as teachers and school leaders, that this is a different relationship that needs careful thought and preparation from the staff we ask to participate.

There's no denying that sex education is hard for lots of us to contemplate teaching: many adults experience awkwardness when talking about sex

205. Pandora Pound, Rebecca Langford and Rona Campbell, "What do young people think about their school-based sex and relationship education? A qualitative synthesis of young people's views and experiences", *BMJ Open*, 6:9, 2016

206. "Nearly three in ten teachers deliver relationships and sex education classes with no training", National Children's Bureau, accessed 2019

with their partner or best friend, never mind a class of 30 teenagers. The reasons that teachers might find sex education difficult include:

- Not knowing what language to use.
- Fear of embarrassment, either their own or the students'.
- Uncertainty about what the students already know and how to pitch their lessons.
- Fear of giving information that could cause upset or anxiousness, or lead to students disclosing sensitive information.[207]
- Strongly held personal views on sex and its place in society, relationships and families.
- Emotional or personal response to sex caused by anything from past trauma to embarrassment.
- Uncertainty about whether students know more than they do – teachers might not want to seem patronising or have a lack of knowledge themselves.
- Lack of training in delivery, so they might be uncertain about the details or low in confidence.
- Fear of behaviour management issues in a different situation.
- Fear of overstepping professional boundaries or that a discussion could get out of hand.

Most of these concerns are quite reasonable, but many can be resolved through better support of teaching staff *before* they deliver RSE lessons. Teachers are as awkward about sex as anyone else and that awkwardness can be compounded by these fears. Training is essential, but so is discussion of these concerns. We need teachers who are confident, so they need support when they don't know how to approach the subject. They shouldn't just be left to read something off a slide, staring at the screen and desperately hoping they aren't asked what a dental dam is for.

207. Teachers should be prepared for this, but it's something that makes many people nervous and disclosures are more likely in certain situations. There may be a training need in terms of what constitutes a disclosure in this kind of lesson – do we report, for example, that students seem "too knowing" about sex, or that they make unexpected comments?

Classroom language

Perhaps more than any other subject, it's impossible to teach sex education without the right language. In some ways, treating it like any other subject can help: the embarrassment can be lessened somewhat if everybody's clear that we are learning and discussing. Children of every age can be required to use the appropriate language, just as they would use basic subject-specific vocabulary anywhere else. Make a list of the words to use. Give them a diagram to label. Test students on it, or discuss the etymology if that helps to familiarise them with the vocabulary. Either way, teachers and students should practise using the correct language.

Using the right names for body parts, and insisting that students know where they're located, can create a little bit of emotional distance. If everyone knows the terms we'll be using in lessons, some of the awkwardness can be removed. In addition, the correct terminology banishes euphemism, which is extremely unhelpful when trying to get students to understand their bodies.

Dr Jessica Taylor is the founder of VictimFocus (set up to challenge the culture of victim-blaming). She tells a story of delivering training in a school where the headteacher told her the staff were all comfortable saying "penis" in lessons, but not "vagina".[208] If necessary (and I'm absolutely serious), teachers delivering RSE could practise saying the words out loud at home – vagina, vulva, penis – until it doesn't feel strange any more. You might feel an idiot at first, but there's something bizarrely liberating about simply chanting the words. I know colleagues who've done the same with students.

The discussion of language can be cathartic and break the ice in the classroom. Start with all the words for genitalia students can think of – they don't have to say them out loud, but can write them in a list or on Post-it notes. Then insist they use the proper anatomical language in class. There are several reasons for this:

---

208. Jessica Taylor, Twitter, 28 August 2019, tinyurl.com/tzfk6ac

- It banishes any uncertainty about how to articulate what you want to discuss.
- As in any other subject, you can't discuss the ideas if you don't have the language.
- The risk of offence is minimised, as is latent homophobia or misogyny often associated with the slang terms.
- It puts everyone on an equal footing – everyone knows what everyone else is talking about.
- It improves behaviour. Euphemisms suggest embarrassment on a teacher's part, which can provide an opportunity for someone to show off and get themselves a little bit more power in the room (often in an effort to hide their own embarrassment).
- Everyone who's having sex should know the basic anatomy of sex – it will be a more pleasurable experience if they understand that there are different bits that do different things!

Teaching fear or pleasure?

The IPPF argues that many sex education programmes perpetuate a sense of fear, focusing almost exclusive on STDs and unwanted pregnancy. In part, this is likely down to a lack of time in the curriculum, but it's also probably to do with discomfort at the idea of teaching students about sexual pleasure. To be clear, I'm not suggesting that we provide detailed instructions on different ways to orgasm. What I am suggesting is that we reinforce the idea that sex can be fun, joyful, an expression of love in an intimate relationship, and an experience that is often unique to the participants involved. It doesn't have to be intimidating, frightening or upsetting. Sex is unpredictable – it might be awkward or even comic – but it shouldn't provoke fear. We do our students a great disservice if we teach sex through such a negative lens.

Many RSE curricula incorporate limited ideas about pleasure, and often from a patriarchal and heteronormative perspective. For example, in sex education starting around puberty, content related to girls' bodies focuses on menstruation, while content related to boys' bodies is concerned with erections, ejaculations and wet dreams. From the earliest lessons, the bodies of boys and men are associated with sexual arousal and pleasure, while the bodies of girls and women are associated with reproduction.[209]

What should we cover in lessons?

1. Sexuality

Under the Equality Act 2010, schools must ensure that the needs of all pupils are met – and this includes delivering same-sex-appropriate education. Many students report that same-sex RSE is lacking and needs dramatic improvement,[210] and that there is a heteronormative bias, perhaps linked with the fact that RSE is mainly aimed at preventing pregnancy. Messages about consent and respect are just as important for same-sex relationships. Students also feel more supported and more confident in coming out if gay and lesbian relationships are a significant part of RSE lessons.[211]

We should also discuss asexuality (lack of sexual feelings and interest in a sexual relationship). An estimated 1% of the population identifies as asexual[212] and that can feel very isolating in a world that seems obsessed with sex. We need to remind students that sexuality is a huge spectrum of feelings and there is a "range of normal", so they understand that all that matters is *their* feelings about sex. It's also entirely possible for teens, like many adults, to feel a lack of sexual desire due to stress, physical or mental lack of fitness, hormonal contraception, and being more attuned to responsive rather than spontaneous desire. By making students aware that all these components integrate with sexuality, we can help them to feel more "normal" and reduce the comparison that leads to anxiousness about sexual relationships.

---

209. *Putting Sexuality Back Into Comprehensive Sexuality Education: making the case for a rights-based, sex-positive approach*, International Planned Parenthood Federation, August 2016

210. *Shh... No Talking: LGBT-inclusive sex and relationships education in the UK*, Terence Higgins Trust, July 2016

211. *Sex and Relationships Education Fit For the 21st Century: we need it now*, Brook, 2011

212. Lucy Wallis, "What is it like to be asexual?", BBC News, 17 January 2012

2. Sexual health and wellbeing

As I've already said, the message many students get from sex education is: do it at your peril. They are told that they risk hideous, permanent disease, or the lonely and unhappy life of a teenage single mother.[213] This is tragic in so many ways. Many STDs are easily treated. Most teenage mothers aren't cast out of the village with a scarlet letter on their dress. It's also tragic because it perpetuates the idea that sex is purely reproductive in nature – and that reduces women to breeding animals or vessels for masculine pleasure.

That's not to say there aren't dangers. STDs can be extremely harmful. Chlamydia, one of the most common, has very few symptoms and can cause long-term health damage. But it's also highly treatable, so it's essential that students know the risks and methods of protection, as well as how to get treatment. At the moment, STDs are a public health issue and rapidly increasing, with 5% more cases in 2018 than 2017.[214] Frighteningly, around 10% of sexually active 16- to 24-year-olds have never used a condom,[215] while almost half said they wouldn't use one with a new partner. A third said carrying one was a sign that someone was promiscuous (a word laden with social judgement). Clearly, the RSE they're currently getting isn't really working.

Discussion about contraceptives needs radical improvement in many schools. Almost nine in 10 women in England who receive contraception from their GP or pharmacy take the pill. A fraction use long-acting reversible contraceptives (Larcs) like the injection, coil and implant, which last between three months and 10 years. Teachers aren't the only ones who don't always provide this information: a quarter of GPs don't offer the implant and just 2% offer the full range of contraceptives.[216] Yet

213. Louisa Allen, "'They think you shouldn't be having sex anyway': young people's suggestions for improving sexuality education content", *Sexualities*, 11:5, 2008

214. *Sexually Transmitted Infections and Screening for Chlamydia in England, 2018*, Public Health England, June 2019

215. Patrick Greenfield, "Half of young people do not use condoms for sex with new partner – poll", *The Guardian*, 15 December 2017

216. "Survey finds worrying gaps in GP contraceptive provision", Family Planning Association, 12 December 2016

Larcs are highly effective and less subject to user error than the pill – they're a genuine option that fewer women know about and can access. The pill, for example, might be 99% effective on perfect use, but studies of its realistic use suggest efficacy of more like 75% over a year. The implant, however, is extremely effective, with just one in 1000 women becoming pregnant over three years of use. Contraceptive choices, when it comes to medical reality, almost always come down to a female-implemented solution.

Women might not insist a condom is used because they want to demonstrate trust to a partner they feel has long-term potential.[217] And they often fear that carrying condoms or suggesting the use of one will make them appear promiscuous. The founders of Hanx, condoms designed "with women in mind", have described the reason they founded their business:

> *"In a chat over lunch, Farah was telling Sarah a story about a friend who had been 'caught' buying condoms by her sniggering (male) boss. It got them thinking that everything about condoms is wrong – overtly masculine, garish and with cringey names. Even today, in a world where our health and wellbeing matter more than ever, men that carry condoms are seen as studs but women are considered one pair of crotchless pants away from a red window in Amsterdam."*[218]

We should encourage the view that carrying condoms is a sign of self-respect and respect for one's partner. We must emphasise that it's perfectly possible to have fun, safe and comfortable sex while wearing one, rather than allowing the myth to flourish that they're horribly inhibiting. There are so many brands, types and thicknesses of condom out there that

---

217. Shayna Skakoon-Sparling and Kenneth M Cramer, "Are we blinded by desire? Relationship motivation and sexual risk-taking intentions during condom negotiation", *Journal of Sex Research*, March 2019

218. "About", hanxofficial.com, accessed 2019

most people simply need to try a variety to find one that works for them. Although there are other types of contraceptive, condoms are really the only option when it comes to STDs.[219] We should teach the importance of using condoms at the beginning of a relationship, but also how to discuss with a partner moving on to something else.

Every method of contraception should be covered in lessons, including their pros and cons and particularly the effect that hormone-based contraceptives can have on women. Boys need to be a part of these conversations, because the decision to have a baby or not should be a joint one and many men aren't aware of the potential impact of hormonal contraceptives. Teaching boys about contraception involves discussion of shared responsibility and respect for one's partner and her health. After all, a condom is the ultimate when it comes to shared responsibility. Either partner can buy, carry and suggest condoms, and they don't have a long-term physical impact on anybody.

Students also need local practical information about how and where to access contraceptives – it's worrying how many students don't realise they can get condoms for free from a medical centre. Studies repeatedly say that free contraception doesn't increase risky sexual behaviour or early sex; in fact, it promotes a healthy and respectful attitude towards sex.[220] Whether gay or straight, students should be encouraged to respect themselves when it comes to sex, and this includes being able to say a particular type of contraceptive is a requirement for them and if they're not comfortable about their partner's response.

We can encourage students to think about when these conversations should happen, too: when is a good time to ask about a condom? From what we learn watching TV and film, the answer is virtually never –

219. There's a fascinating article on non-Western responses to female condoms, which points out that while their take-up in the UK is basically zero, in countries where men are traditionally averse to wearing condoms, female condoms are literally lifesavers: Kate Burt, "Whatever happened to the Femidom?", *The Guardian*, 23 August 2005

220. Gina M Secura, Tiffany Adams, Christina M Buckel, Qiuhong Zhao and Jeffrey F Peipert, "Change in sexual behaviour with provision of no-cost contraception", *Obstetrics and Gynecology*, 124:1, July 2014

contraception is almost non-existent on-screen. A 2005 study found that in the top 200 films of all time, there was just one mention of contraception.[221] And although soaps are a little more likely to feature some discussion, it usually centres around the embarrassment of trying to buy condoms. It's usually women who have to deal with any negative consequences of sex, particularly pregnancy, where male characters are absolved of responsibility either through refusing to become involved, or because the female thinks she must "deal with it" alone – another dangerously gendered message.

The picture hasn't improved much in the past decade. In 2017, a host of media stories were published about contestants on *Love Island* not having safe sex and requesting emergency contraception (interestingly, few of the stories were critical of the broadcaster's decision to show the sex on-screen). A 2019 study of on-screen sex found that just 2% of films showed or even implied condom use.[222] Any teenagers turning to pop culture for support about contraception will receive dangerous messages.

3. Sexual rights
Sexual rights include the right to express one's sexuality freely and without prejudice, as well as the right to be free from sexual coercion and control. An animation released by Thames Valley Police likens sexual consent to making someone a cup of tea; this may sound flippant, but the video went viral for the brilliance and clarity of its message. If someone says no, don't make them tea! If someone's unconscious, don't make them tea and don't force them to drink it![223] Ideally, consent is given in a conversation that goes something like this:

221. Hasantha Gunasekera, Simon Chapman and Sharon Campbell, "Sex and drugs in popular movies: an analysis of the top 200 films", *Journal of the Royal Society of Medicine*, 98:10, October 2005

222. *Sex on Screen: how realistic is it?*, Zava, 2019

223. Emmeline May at RockStarDinosaurPiratePrincess and Blue Seat Studios, *Tea and Consent*, Thames Valley Police, 2015

"Shall we have sex now? Is that what you want?"
"Yes, I'd like full sex now."
"Great. Me as well."

And when both participants are alcohol- and drug-free, everyone proceeds pretty happily. But, as adults, we recognise that it's not always that clear-cut. Alcohol and drugs can cloud the issue, and we should discuss with students why being intoxicated might make consent impossible. We need to be brave and have difficult conversations about being drunk, and how you might want sex in the moment that you go on to regret in the morning and that you'd never have consented to sober. Where is the line in that situation? Not only is a drunk person less able to give consent, but they're also less able to interpret signals of consent from others.[224] We need students to understand the legal and ethical positions, and to be able to think critically about consent long before they get a drink in their hand. Equally, we need to discuss the signals of consent, because although kissing and touching aren't automatic signs of consent for sex, many people use them as such (perfectly willingly and consensually). In sexual relationships, we want people to have the confidence to say no if they feel uncomfortable, and to be able to have a clear and direct conversation about consent if they're unsure what someone's body is telling them.

Students need to learn about taking responsibility for themselves and others. There are simply some people in the world who are criminal and opportunist, and if we accept that we lock our front doors and our cars against theft, then we should avoid making ourselves vulnerable and putting ourselves into frightening situations. We need to guard against people who will take advantage in a criminal and threatening way. The aim of such discussions isn't to frighten or intimidate, but to explore the differences in what is a very complex understanding of consent. We also need to emphasise that victims don't deserve what may happen to them, and to avoid victim-blaming in conversations about responsible behaviour.

---

224. "Consent and alcohol", Family Planning Association, accessed 2019

Just as we want students to be confident in discussing contraception, we want them to be able to talk about consent in the same way. We want them to decide – long before the critical moment arises – when they think is the right time to talk about sex with a potential partner, to talk about contraception and STD testing, and to talk about what it might mean to each of them to have sex. If we give them safe spaces and guidance in thinking about this, they can make those decisions for themselves, which will make it easier for them to proceed confidently when it really matters.

4. Sex positivity

A sex-positive curriculum isn't about promoting sex or teaching young people how to have sex. Rather, it's about tackling taboos to make sure that fear, shame and guilt don't shroud the discussions. It's really important to emphasise that everyone's body is normal. The Labia Library online, for example, presents dozens of pictures of women's labia, all different, in order to send the message that worrying about our bodies during sex isn't necessary and can be harmful to our self-esteem and sexual experience (the photographer Laura Dodsworth has completed a similar project). Sure, pictures of labia have the potential to make staff and students uncomfortable, but the point is that if everyone's hands are different, of course this applies to every part of your body. A sex-positive curriculum celebrates sexuality as a part of life that should bring happiness and energy, not shame and self-criticism.

5. Pleasure

This may well be the most difficult discussion for many teachers and the place where professional neutrality can be most important. The areas to be explored here are how to find your own pleasure and how to have the confidence and trust in your relationships to experiment, explore and ask for what you want. Trust is hugely underrated in sex education, yet trust in a partner is a major factor in a healthy sex life and attitude, so students have to be able to question and define what trust means to them. This is the "relationships" bit of relationships and sex education, as we explore the context of sex. According to the sex educator Emily

Nagoski, "context – your external circumstances and your present mental state – is as crucial to your sexual wellbeing as your body and your brain".[225] Context includes: trust in the relationship; body self-image and self-confidence; confidence in your own experiences and those of your partner; expectations; personal safety; emotional connection; stress; and other factors that can affect a person's thinking. Understanding the issue of context can dismantle some of the socially imposed barriers of expectation that rest on young women and men when they're thinking about sex.

Here is another place where, particularly for older secondary students, it might be useful to think of RSE as more like an academic subject. Just as you might use sources or textbooks there, you can use sources and reference books in RSE to create a space for discussion at a professional distance. Writers like Emily Nagoski are highly articulate and accessible, though there are also plenty of books aimed specifically at teenagers.

Teaching about pornography

Porn is a major concern for parents and teachers when it comes to teens' sexuality. According to the National Union of Students, 29% of students (sixth form and university) have used porn to learn about sex, despite 73% saying they know it creates unrealistic expectations.[226] That means, among other things, that a quarter *don't* think what they see in porn is unrealistic. And younger children are accessing porn. A study found that half of 11- to 16-year-olds in the UK had seen online porn, and almost all of those children had seen it by the age of 14. Of those who had seen porn, more than a third wanted to repeat things they'd seen on-screen.[227]

---

225. Emily Nagoski, *Come As You Are: the surprising new science that will transform your sex life*, Scribe, 2015

226. *Student Opinion Survey: November 2014*, National Union of Students

227. Elena Martellozzo, Andy Monaghan, Joanna R Adler, Julia Davidson, Rodolfo Leyva and Miranda AH Horvath, *'I Wasn't Sure it was Normal to Watch It': a quantitative and qualitative examination of the impact of online pornography on the values, attitudes, beliefs and behaviours of children and young people*, Middlesex University London, June 2016

Students who are exposed to this content earlier are more likely to start sexual activity earlier, and are more likely to have casual, unprotected sex.[228] There are also concerns about the violent pornography that children can access; one woman in the UK is strangled to death by her partner every two weeks and, frequently, those killings are associated with the prevalence of choking as sex play in relatively mainstream pornography.[229] Watching pornography doesn't automatically turn children into abusers, but regular viewing creates different expectations, desensitises them to what is fun and what is damaging, and makes violent sex seem sexier.[230] The more young people watch porn, the more likely they are in later life to report sexual dysfunction, including the inability to become aroused without it.[231]

Yet another difficult topic! How do we talk about pornography with students without frightening them and demonising their natural curiosity? Presenting the facts can be helpful. Use source documents, articles and research, scaffolded as needed. Many teenagers, boys and girls, will be watching porn and have questions associated with it. Offer a safe space for them to ask these questions, either in a pastoral support session or via a box accessible to all, where students can post their questions anonymously and have them answered in the next lesson.

Teacher and parental support

One of the big concerns with the RSE curriculum is how parents will respond. How to avoid overstepping the line between school and home?

---

228. Carolyn C Ross, "Overexposed and under-prepared: the effects of early exposure to sexual content", *Psychology Today*, 13 August 2012

229. Anna Moore and Coco Khan, "The fatal, hateful rise of choking during sex", *The Guardian*, 25 July 2019

230. Elena Martellozzo, Andy Monaghan, Joanna R Adler, Julia Davidson, Rodolfo Leyva and Miranda AH Horvath, *'I Wasn't Sure it was Normal to Watch It': a quantitative and qualitative examination of the impact of online pornography on the values, attitudes, beliefs and behaviours of children and young people*, Middlesex University London, June 2016

231. Jonathan Berger, Andrew Doan, John Kehoe, Michael Marshall, Warren Klam, Donald Crain and Matthew Christman, "Survey of sexual function and pornography", *Journal of Urology*, 197:4, April 2017

Parents should not only be on board, but also confident themselves. The curriculum needs to be communicated effectively, alongside the resources we use and the support and information available to them as well. The curriculum intent should be clear: to empower students to have a happy, healthy and emotionally strong life, recognising the role that sexuality plays in physical, mental and reproductive health; and to ensure that students are able to be safe, self-confident and demonstrate respect for themselves and others. Most parents feel supported rather than challenged when schools get involved with more comprehensive sex education, with many thinking that schools cover more than they do.[232]

---

232. *Sex and Relationships Education Fit For the 21st Century: we need it now,* Brook, 2011

- Is RSE delivered by confident subject specialists, or by whoever has space on their timetable? Is this a reasonable and good delivery mechanism? What training and discussion is available to non-subject specialists?
- Is RSE is integrated across the PSHE curriculum (and beyond, where appropriate), rather than "dealt with" in one-off lessons? If one-offs are unavoidable, are there opportunities for follow-up?
- Is RSE taught in a positive and supportive way, enabling students to engage in discussion and ask questions?
- Do students have questioning opportunities, either in lessons or via mechanisms like anonymous question boxes?
- Is the language used in RSE positive, reassuring and inclusive? Do teachers need language training to ensure everyone is confident and knowledgeable when it comes to discussing sex and bodies?
- Are you incorporating a range of views, representing all sexualities and, in short, avoiding a narrow heteronormative perspective?
- If you personally don't teach sex education, are discussions in your subject open, thoughtful and inclusive as well? Or is sex often presented negatively, or as simply a biological need?

FURTHER RESOURCES

Putting Sexuality Back Into Comprehensive Sexuality Education is an
International Planned Parenthood Federation report containing a series of
recommendations on implementing sex-positivity into RSE. *bit.ly/33Y0koW*

Sexual Attitude and Lifestyles in Britain, an excellent infographic on the 2010–12
National Survey of Sexual Attitudes and Lifestyles, can provoke interesting
discussion. *natsal.ac.uk/media/2102/natsal-infographic.pdf*

What Is Asexuality? This website provides information and discussion on what
it is to be asexual and some of the concerns associated with it.
whatisasexuality.com

13. Periods

Tampon commercial, detergent commercial, maxipad commercial, Windex commercial. You'd think all women do is clean and bleed – Gillian Flynn, *Gone Girl*

Historically, menstrual blood has been considered disgusting (and somehow different to other blood). Periods have been seen as some sort of mystical force, and women have been subjected to isolation and restriction during menstruation. These attitudes "other" women and turn periods into something to be either feared or revered, instead of something that is simply human. With the potential physical effects ranging from the less severe (weight gain, irritability, soreness, insomnia) to the more debilitating (acute pain or uncontrollable mood swings),[233] every woman's experience of menstruation is slightly different and changes throughout her lifetime. Women's health also seems to be taken less seriously when it comes to periods. The tennis player Serena Williams, suffering from menstrual migraines, was told there was nothing wrong with her – she just *thought* there was.[234]

---

233. "Periods: overview", NHS, accessed 2019

234. Katie Whyatt, "Steph Houghton right to tackle period poverty on national TV, but women athletes deserve much more on the issue", *The Telegraph*, 13 August 2019

Period poverty might be more talked about at the moment, but the day-to-day experience of periods is often censored – literally, in many cases. In 2015, Instagram repeatedly deleted an image by the poet Rupi Kaur of a fully clothed woman lying on a bed with a bloodstain between her legs.[235] Etsy and Facebook have banned shops and advertising of art that celebrates menstruation, describing it as "adult" content and therefore "inappropriate".[236]

Schools are required to teach children about menstruation and "menstrual wellbeing" by the end of primary school, but the details of what that involves are pretty vague.[237] It's a shameful statistic that one in seven girls have reported not knowing what was happening when their first period started.[238] Even when they are told some of the details and the biology, they often don't really know what to expect. Worse, 79% have experiences that concern them and 12% have actually been told not to discuss their periods with their mother. Nearly half are embarrassed to discuss menstruation – with anybody.[239] So we potentially have a huge number of girls who don't understand what's happening to their bodies and what they could – or should – be doing to manage it. Information from friends or online isn't necessarily accurate or helpful, and can perpetuate myths that make girls feel unclean or ashamed. We should be worried about these statistics. They reveal a culture of shame and taboo associated with periods from a very young age. We need to challenge this with girls and with boys.

Girls usually start their periods at around 12,[240] so they're an important part of secondary school life, yet everything around them tells

235. Tish Weinstock, "Why did Instagram delete this image of a woman on her period?" *i-D*, 10 April 2015

236. Sanjana Chowhan, "The (very) puritanical online censorship of periods", *The Establishment*, 23 August 2016

237. *Relationships Education, Relationships and Sex Education (RSE) and Health Education*, Department for Education, 2019

238. *Break the Barriers: girls' experiences of menstruation in the UK*, Plan International UK, January 2018

239. Ibid.

240. "Periods: overview", NHS, accessed 2019

girls not to speak to anyone about menstruation. Although the biology is covered in class, the surrounding taboos and realities are more often "picked up" rather than actually discussed. Periods are often treated squeamishly or silently. Girls pull their jumper sleeves down to hide their tampons, feeling ashamed of what they're leaving the room to do. In an average school with around 700 female students, we could assume that roughly 160 are experiencing menstruation in any given week (based on an average cycle of 28 days). But when I asked on Twitter, few teachers had seen girls openly carrying tampons and around half had seen girls hiding them. A quarter had never seen a girl with a sanitary product.

Women spend approximately 35 years menstruating and pay as much as £18,000 for menstrual products over a lifetime. This is why so many girls experience period poverty, when they're unable to afford sanitary products like towels or tampons, so end up either reusing them (which is not only physically uncomfortable and unpleasant, but also potentially dangerous) or using something else, like socks or toilet roll. Research has shown that more than 137,700 girls have missed school because of period poverty and one in 10 can't afford menstrual products. Periods have an impact in lessons, too, with 68% of girls reporting being unable to concentrate because of issues such as pain, cramps or other discomfort, the fear of leaking or the fear of not being allowed to go to the bathroom.

How we can help

We need a two-step approach to periods in schools. The first step is to practically support girls in learning about their bodies and how to recognise, accept and manage their periods. The second is to actively work to remove the shame and stigma surrounding periods, so that students can freely discuss them.

Some young people are confidently leading the way. The Twitter poll I carried out also elicited several stories of girls standing up to shaming, calling out those who used "Are you on your period?" as an insult, or openly carrying sanitary products to the toilet. I also heard many stories of teachers keeping products in their desk drawers, with some almost comic "secret networks" in which girls were encouraged to "spread the word" that supplies were available. Although I think it's fantastic that these teachers are supportive, I believe it's a whole-school responsibility to ensure there are options for students.

The Department for Education's statutory guidance for RSE (2020) contains a paragraph on its requirements for teaching about menstruation, which are primarily focused on the physical details:

> *"The onset of menstruation can be confusing or even alarming for girls if they are not prepared. Pupils should be taught key facts about the menstrual cycle including what is an average period, range of menstrual products and the implications for emotional and physical health. In addition to curriculum content, schools should also make adequate and sensitive arrangements to help girls prepare for and manage menstruation including with requests for menstrual products."*[241]

Many girls will have started their periods before leaving primary school, so it's essential that they're taught the essentials by then. As they enter key stage 3, we can encourage a more holistic focus on how reproductive health contributes to their wellbeing, as well as the biology. Covering these ideas at KS3 is important, because teenage girls' cycles can change regularly and they need to learn the science of how their body works.

Confidence comes from knowledge

Girls need to be empowered to explore and pay attention to what's normal for them, as well as understanding the normal range. For many, periods vary from one cycle to the next and girls need to know this; they also need to be able to recognise any effects that fall outside the norm, like extreme pain. We should be talking about reproductive health in a positive and factual way. This should include encouraging girls to track some of their own experiences, such as how long their cycles and periods

---

241. *Relationships Education, Relationships and Sex Education (RSE) and Health Education*, Department for Education, 2019

are, and their general patterns of mood and body.[242] A simple monthly tracker, recording dates of bleeding alongside common factors like mood, pain, sleep and so on, can be very useful for girls. Tracking is also a step towards being able to manage their periods and begin to predict their cycles.

Sharing some of these trackers, anonymously, would be an incredibly powerful way to make it clear to young women that "normal" is a huge range, as well as the fact that a woman's cycle changes regularly. Girls need to learn what normal is *for them*, so that they can feel comfortable in their bodies and seek help if needed. Being a teenager is difficult enough emotionally, but understanding that on some days your body or mood is different because your period is due in three days can bring some comfort.

Menstrual policies in school

Access to sanitary products is essential. Since early 2020, funding has been available for primary schools to provide free menstrual supplies,[243] which begins to address period poverty and the pupil absences caused by it. But how and when these products are provided requires careful thought.

It seems, from discussions with teachers whose schools provide products, that the most common approach is for supplies to be held by heads of year or office staff. Personally, I think this is the wrong solution. Even assuming that those people are always available, there's still a balance to be struck between working to remove the stigma of periods and accepting that students won't always want to go to an office to pick up a tampon. There's also the hassle involved. If you're in the loo and realise you've started your period, you don't want to have to attempt

242. There is a current trend of using fertility tracking apps as a way to prevent pregnancy, avoiding sex or "pulling out" on the most fertile days, perhaps because of a wariness of hormonal contraception. Around 31% of young American women have used "natural contraception methods" in a similar way. It's worth challenging the use of these methods, as they are pretty unreliable and, of course, don't protect against STDs

243. "Free sanitary products in all primary schools", Department for Education, 16 April 2019

to mop up, then track down your head of year (whose office could be anywhere in the school), go back to the loo and finally head back to your lesson, where your teacher will no doubt ask what took you so long.

Girls need to be able to access products when and where they need them. Put a box in the toilet that contains a range of tampons, towels, even spare underwear if possible, so that girls can be confident that they're covered.

Alternative products are also worth discussing, particularly as they're currently less familiar. Menstrual cups are increasing in popularity: they are more environmentally friendly and sustainable, and although they cost about £15–20 to buy, they are far, far cheaper in the long run, because they don't need to be replaced for several years. Research has suggested that they may be safer than tampons: they interfere less with the vagina's natural lubrication and bacteria, thus causing fewer infections.[244] Although it takes a little practice to get used to inserting them, they're just as comfortable and long-lasting as tampons. They're also perfectly usable at school.

Toilet policies in schools must recognise the unpredictability of periods. Even if you track your cycles and know your period is likely to show up sometime in the day, you can't predict when and you can't predict how much you'll bleed. Teenagers are also more likely than adults to have irregular cycles.[245] Periods can be very distracting, so surely it's better for a student to miss five minutes of the lesson to go to the loo and change their product than to spend half an hour worrying about leaking and the discomfort of having ruined underwear for the rest of the day? This applies to staff as well: periods can continue to be challenging for many women throughout their menstruating lives, and teachers are sometimes even more trapped in the classroom than students.

This is the reality for many women. Periods are hard to judge. We need to design toilet policies with empathy, recognising that teenagers

244. Anna Maria van Eijk, Garazi Zulaika, Madeline Lenchner, Linda Mason, Muthusamy Sivakami, Elizabeth Nyothach, Holger Unger, Kayla Laserson and Penelope A Phillips-Howard, "Menstrual cup use, leakage, acceptability, safety, and availability: a systematic review and meta-analysis", *The Lancet*, 4:8, August 2019

245. Anna Druet, "What is an 'irregular' menstrual cycle?", *Clue*, 18 November 2018

are just learning how to manage their periods and will sometimes be taken by surprise. We don't want to give complete free rein: I've known girls who have claimed "women's things" to get out of a lesson when bored, or pulled a tampon from their bag to shock a male teacher, or said they're entitled to chocolate right this moment because they're on. Taking advantage like this isn't OK, but such incidents are far less frequent than the embarrassment suffered by so many girls. Whole-school awareness of who is requesting permission to leave lessons and when can be helpful. We might be able spot patterns: always going to the toilet during her least favourite lesson, for example. Or, if a girl is regularly going to the toilet during lessons, we might offer some suggestions on how she could manage her period differently – it might be an indication that she doesn't have access to sanitary products and needs some support.

Tackling taboos

To normalise periods, we need to explore the origins of the taboos surrounding them. Some are rooted in fears about uncleanliness or about a woman's strength being sapped during menstruation, making her somehow incapable. The representation of periods can also contribute to shame and anxiousness – they're barely mentioned in the media, in literature, on TV or in film. Although mentions have increased in the past couple of years, alongside a growing awareness of period poverty, most media ignore them almost completely, unless joking about them or pointing out how disgusting they are. The alternative is that menstruation is elevated into something horrifyingly potent. From *Carrie* onwards, periods have been depicted as a gaining of power through sexuality and treated as grotesque. Although some writers attempt to reclaim menstruation as a female strength, this plays into the stereotype that sexuality is a woman's primary power: by having her period she has become somehow "other"; she's temporarily unavailable to men and needs to be treated differently.

Periods are also a go-to way to put females down. If a woman is angry or upset, remarks about being "on the blob" are ubiquitous, as evidenced when I asked on Twitter if anyone had witnessed period-related conversations or banter – they were mostly aimed at students, male and female, and some at staff. Such comments are often delivered at the moment when women demonstrate some "unfeminine" behaviour, like showing an unacceptable emotion too strongly or speaking up when they've been told to be silent. This language should be challenged as misogynistic and considered part of sexist bullying. It needs to be discussed as soon as it's used, just as we would challenge any slur related to sexuality or ethnicity. Teenagers don't always realise that they're being misogynistic, so we need encourage dialogue about why and how these taboos have arisen, recognising that they are part of an effort to keep women in a weakened position.

Language check

Like so much related to women and women's health, metaphors and euphemisms abound when it comes to periods. Many of them either ultra-feminise women or focus on the gruesome and disgusting. As teachers, our language should be about menstruation, periods and vaginas – biological terms that we should be comfortable using and our students comfortable hearing. We have to challenge young people who use period-related language in a derogatory way.

Discussing the words that students use can unlock conversations about shame, fear and lack of knowledge. My go-to for a language debate of this sort is always to list the descriptions and then categorise them; it's pretty shocking to see them all written down and realise how much the language reveals about the revulsion people feel towards periods.

Much discussion of periods also talks about "symptoms", a word that medicalises menstruation and implies something abnormal or diseased. An alternative would be discussing *experiences* of menstruation, acknowledging that in 10 different periods there will likely be 10 different experiences. By changing the language that we use to describe menstruation, we can start to break down the taboos.

—————— AUDIT QUESTIONS ——————

- Does induction for new students include information on how to access sanitary products in a way that normalises it?
- Are sanitary products freely available without students having to speak to staff?
- Are students able to go to the bathroom without question? If not, have the period implications of the policy been considered?
- Are staff able to take regular toilet breaks?
- Is menstruation taught in a way that associates it with students' health and wellbeing, encourages familiarity with their own bodies and presents different experiences of "normal"?
- Are taboos, misconceptions and myths addressed in lessons?
- Are absences tracked for patterns possibly related to periods, so that support can be provided to struggling students?
- Are teachers fully prepared and supported in teaching about menstruation?
- Check your language: do lessons refer to "symptoms"? Do teachers use the words "menstruation" and "vagina"? Is derogatory language challenged and explored in the classroom and outside it?

FURTHER RESOURCES

Dr Anita Mitra is a gynaecologist offering podcasts and a blog that answers a multitude of questions. She gives very open, clear and accessible advice. *gynaegeek.com*

Emily Nagoski is a sex educator and author of the excellent *Come As You Are*. Her website hosts her very accessible TED talks on shame and body confidence (aimed at adult audiences, so be aware of the cohort). She's particularly good at discussing how the concept of "normal" contributes to bodily shame. *emilynagoski.com*

Endometriosis UK provides useful resources for teenage girls on what periods are like, in addition to specific information on endometriosis. *endometriosis-uk.org*

14. Overcoming perfectionism

Done is better than perfect – Sheryl Sandberg

"Perfectionism" is a term that is strangely overused and underused at the same time. It's a classic interview humblebrag: "What's your worst quality?" "Oh, I'm a perfectionist." People use it to convey that they like to get things right or work hard. But, at the same time, teenagers in particular chronically under-recognise it in themselves; they can't understand why their brain is behaving in this way that seemingly stops them achieving what they want to.

For the "good girl" we considered in Part I, her self-worth is tied up in messy and difficult knots to the value that others place on her. She seeks approval from others to feel good about herself, and when she doesn't have that validation, she can feel worthless. When she feels worthwhile only in very specific circumstances, she can quickly reduce her behaviours to just those activities.

Having high standards is one thing. But perfectionism is setting standards so high that they can't be met, at least not without extreme difficulty. Perfectionists get anxious about mistakes, and rather than accepting them as part of learning and moving on, they will do pretty much anything to avoid making them. They're afraid of looking stupid, which is one of the worst things in their world; they're afraid of making a fool of themselves, or being thought a horrible, worthless person because of their mistake. The desire to please and be perfect is overwhelming, to the point where they take hours to complete a simple task, or they don't do it at all because they're frightened to put pen to paper.

It's important to know that perfectionism isn't simply about wanting to do well. That's too weak a statement. It's almost the opposite: the fear of failing to be perfect or excellent is so intense that it becomes a symbol of the self. Failure means the person is bad or worthless. Perfectionism isn't just about wanting to perfect things like jobs, tasks or relationships; it's fundamentally about wanting to perfect yourself. When those aspirations aren't met, the result is exaggerated and punitive self-criticism.

An alternative type of perfectionism is where "individuals believe their social context is excessively demanding, that others judge them harshly, and that they must display perfection to secure approval".[246] The two kinds are often deeply intertwined.

As you'd expect, there are a range of complex factors behind perfectionism, including:

- Social media's impact on body image.
- A narrowing public perception of education that focuses on its importance only in relation to work.
- A social definition of success as linked with money and acquisition, rather than a broader definition of happiness.
- An expectation that "being happy" means feeling joyful all the time.
- An increasing belief that society is a meritocracy. If you work hard, you'll succeed, but the flip side is also true: if you fail, it's your own fault.[247]

246. Thomas Curran and Andrew P Hill, "Perfectionism is increasing over time: a meta-analysis of birth cohort differences from 1989 to 2016", *Psychological Bulletin*, 145:4, 2019
247. Ibid.

Perfectionism is more common in girls and women. It doesn't stop when we leave school, either. A frequently cited study found that women don't apply for jobs unless they feel they meet every criterion (men, on the other hand, will on average apply if they meet 60% of the criteria).[248] A further study suggested this was only partly due to internal perfectionism, or lack of belief that they could do the job, and partly to do with external perfectionism – the belief that others wouldn't hire them because they weren't perfect.

Perfectionism is strongly linked to other mental health problems, particularly eating disorders in girls.[249] Anorexia nervosa[250] and bulimia[251] both have strong correlations to perfectionism, which is often evident before the eating disorder presents itself. Awareness of developing perfectionism has been suggested as a targeted intervention for treating eating disorders.[252] It's a complex connection, but certainly eating disorders are compounded by perfectionism in other aspects of life, typically linked with achievement and academic success.

Girls also suffer because there are such conflicting narratives about what "success" and "perfection" entail. The narrative of economic success conflicts with the narrative of nurturing success in family life as

248. Tara Sophia Mohr, "Why women don't apply for jobs unless they're 100% qualified", *Harvard Business Review*, 25 August 2014

249. Anna M Bardone-Cone, Stephen A Wonderlich, Randy O Frost, Cynthia M Bulik, James E Mitchell, Saritha Uppala and Heather Simonich, "Perfectionism and eating disorders: current status and future directions", *Clinical Psychology Review*, 27:3, April 2007

250. Katherine A Halmi, Dara Bellace, Samantha Berthod, Samiran Ghosh, Wade Berrettini, Harry A Brandt, Cynthia M Bulik, Steve Crawford, Manfred M Fichter, Craig L Johnson, Allan Kaplan, Walter H Kaye, Laura Thornton, Janet Treasure, D Blake Woodside and Michael Strober, "An examination of early childhood perfectionism across anorexia nervosa subtypes", *International Journal of Eating Disorders*, 45:6, September 2012

251. Ivy-Lee L Kehayes, Martin M Smith, Simon B Sherry, Vanja Vidovic and Donald H Saklofske, "Are perfectionism dimensions risk factors for bulimic symptoms? A meta-analysis of longitudinal studies", *Personality and Individual Differences*, 138, February 2019

252. Samantha Lloyd, Jenny Yiend, Ulrike Schmidt and Kate Tchanturia, "Perfectionism in anorexia nervosa: novel performance based evidence", *PLoS ONE*, 9:10, October 2014

a mother. Perfectionism also – often and to a point – works in teachers' favour in education. We *want* perfect students. We like neat students with pretty coloured annotations and tidily stuck-in sheets. We want students who strive to be the best. Where is the line between useful revision planning and perfectionism? Or between students striving to get a good grade and placing all their self-worth on their results?

Perfectionism, particularly in more expressive areas like writing and art, can be caused by having better taste than ability, so model answers need to be carefully constructed to show what will improve students' work but is still within their reach. When we know what good writing, drawing or photography is but can't achieve it, it's very frustrating. Students with perfectionist tendencies can lack the resilience to see their abilities improving towards that standard, only seeing the gap between the two.

In my lessons, creative writing is often a flashpoint for my students, but perfectionism happens in every aspect of the subjects I teach. Sometimes I say something about my own writing:

> *"I get it. You hate what you've written. In fact, it's like you hate it so much you want to set it on fire, and the pen you wrote it with, and then throw the ashes into the wind so it's completely and utterly destroyed, because you can't believe you've written something so horrifically bad and just want to obliterate it."*

Now, I'm a pretty decent fiction writer with plenty of practice and training, all the way up to an MA and some publications. But I still feel this way sometimes, as do most fiction writers at some point. I can't bear the idea of creating something that isn't any good. The thought of letting someone see it can make me feel physically sick, and can also cause intense anger that feels like it's externally directed but isn't really. Overcoming this is really intense and difficult. A lot of the time I slip back, as many people with anxiety-related issues do. No progress is linear. But the strategies I outline in this chapter have all aided me immensely and continue to help me to be productive, happy and to achieve in my professional and personal life.

Perfectionist behaviours

In the classroom, the following behaviours can have their roots in perfectionist thinking. Everyone does some of these some of the time, but repeated examples might indicate a problem:

- **Procrastination**. Not completing work can have many causes, but persistent procrastination or trouble getting started can be down to perfectionism.
- **Excessive neatness**. Recutting paper to tidy it up, glueing with a ruler to keep it straight, drawing font-like headers for the title, spending ages with Tipp-Ex, heavily scoring out a mistake so it can't be seen – perfectionism can be behind all of these.
- **Redoing things**. Examples include wanting new sheets or booklets because they've made a mistake, or developing a habit of going home and rewriting work. Writing in pencil often suggests they're afraid of making mistakes, especially if they want to go over the work in pen later. Such repetition isn't very useful for revision – usually it's to make themselves feel better.
- **Handwriting**. I'm all for legible handwriting, but paying more attention to the look of handwriting than to the content can be a warning sign. Refusal to write in cursive "because it looks messy" is also a sign of perfectionism – print has become seen as "neat".
- **Spending too long on homework**. Always spending more hours than needed on a piece of work, or spending a disproportionate amount of time compared with the rest of the class, could be a cause for concern.
- **Inability to make simple decisions**. This is most obvious when students don't know how to start their work, or feel unable to choose the right word.
- **Inability to write or speak without rehearsal**. Plenty of girls would go through school in virtual silence, rather than raise their hand and

make a mistake. They might be unable to give verbal responses, or even to write short tasks, without planning first. For a perfectionist, the idea of being called on is close to agonising. There's the fear of giving the wrong answer, of someone laughing or criticising, of stumbling over your words, of ending up embarrassed. So many girls spend lessons dreading class discussion and trying to avoid eye contact, instead of thinking about the answers.

Self-punishment is also common, though we might not notice it as easily. When they inevitably fall short of their own expectations, they punish themselves, often by denying themselves something – food, stress relief, relaxation, friendship. "I didn't finish this, so I have to stay in all weekend and work." "I didn't work out, so I can't eat dinner tonight."

Types of perfectionist thinking

Perfectionism manifests in different ways, but at heart they are all about being unable to live up to an internalised standard.[253]

- **Black and white thinking**: anything less than full marks (perfection!) is a failure. If I need help, I'm not doing well enough. If I can't do it, I can't learn how.
- **Catastrophic thinking**: I won't be able to cope if I can't get this right. If I can't learn this, I'll fail the exam. If I get the speaking assessment wrong, everyone will laugh and I'll be humiliated.
- **Probability overestimation**: I won't do well even though I spent days preparing. I can't not go in, everyone will think I'm weak.
- **Should(n't) statements**: I shouldn't be making that mistake. I should have seen that answer. I should know that.

Perfectionists are unlikely to be able to self-soothe effectively. Instead, pretty much all their self-talk will be overwhelmingly criticism and threat.

---

253. "How to overcome perfectionism", Anxiety Canada, accessed 2019

Challenging perfectionism

I'll look at overcoming procrastination in a moment, because it's the indicator most teachers will notice first, but these strategies can help students in other areas:

- **Ask them what someone else would do**. It can be useful to think from the perspective of someone who loves you and has your back. Ask your student, "What would your best friend tell you?" Encourage them to practise the best-friend approach rather than listening to their self-criticism.
- **Set clear and realistic expectations**. We don't expect a GCSE essay to read like an undergraduate's, or a Year 7 student to know everything about Aristotelian tragedy or the complexities of wave theory. It's important to convey realistic expectations with appropriate challenge; we want students to be happy and confident in their learning. Part of that is understanding what's possible with the time and ability available to them. Using genuine models is very helpful, but we also need to remember when writing our own that it should set an attainable standard for the students we teach.
- **Ask how much time they think is needed for the task**. Particularly for homework or a timed task, ask students to estimate the time it will take and work with them to make it realistic. For example, a 45-minute exam essay might take 90 minutes at first if you need to research, plan, write and edit. But the more practice you have, the closer you can get to the 45 minutes.
- **Give time estimates for homework**. It helps perfectionists to have boundaries and know the expectations of others; this includes time and what they're expected to produce within it.
- **Share the difficulty**. Finding something challenging is better if you're supposed to. It's comforting for students when we say that this is beyond what they've done before, because it legitimises the struggle. It's when they find it hard and think they shouldn't that problems can develop.

- **Recast statements with positive and realistic language**. We recast students' language all the time to model academic vocabulary. We should recast their limiting self-beliefs in the same way. Examples of positive realism:

  Nobody is perfect.
  Mistakes are common in exam situations.
  It's OK to feel angry or upset.
  It's OK if you're having a bad day.
  This is challenging stuff, which can be frustrating.

  But we have to mean it, and back it up with positive and warm classroom relationships. It's not about letting them off – we expect the work to be done and done well. But we expect it to be done realistically, too.
- **Encourage imperfection.** What level of imperfection are they/we willing to tolerate? Open discussion of what could be left undone can be helpful.
- **Share examples of drafting**. Not just teacher modelling, although that's valuable, too. But, in poetry, we can use first-draft edits from writers like Sylvia Plath or Wilfred Owen (biographies and the British Library are good sources), or in art we can use preparatory sketches.
- **Exposure practice.** Practising deliberately making "mistakes" is a way to calm the anxiousness that occurs when they happen for real. It might be challenging for us as teachers to instruct students to do less than "their best", but it can be the best long-term strategy for perfectionists. Encourage them to deliberately cut something less than straight, or speak without internal rehearsal. They need to learn through experience that they won't get into trouble, fail or be told they're stupid if they make mistakes or (as they see it) slack off a little. In fact, it'll set them up for more productive and happy working routines that are balanced and stress-free. Exposure practice is very emotionally

challenging. It really should be little and often; too much can become threatening and cause more damage. And it needs to be frequently repeated to "overwrite" perfectionist habits.

- **Help students to prioritise**. Most schools help students to work on homework routines, for example, but we should also discuss how to prioritise in challenging situations. When you realise that you're achieving in English but not geography, shouldn't you allocate your time differently? When you've run out of time, how do you decide what to do? How do you decide what's essential?
- **Reward**. When someone overcomes their perfectionism, they should be celebrated. Reward effort, creativity and risk-taking even if it doesn't result in excellent work. Reward spending the estimated time on a task rather than overrunning. Reward individuality and being different.
- **Empathise**. I share my feelings about creative writing because they are extreme, and because many of the girls I teach feel the same, but won't say so because it *is* extreme to feel this way.
- **Keep talking about the impossibility of models in the wider world**. Regularly challenge the views or expectations that students encounter. Help them to continue to recognise the impossible – and homogeneous – expectations placed on them.

Overcoming procrastination

Now let's look at some strategies that can help students to conquer procrastination:

- Create a relaxed environment. Expectations can be high without activating the threat drive. Remove distractions as far as possible: silence can be the most useful way to do this, but ensure students can ask for guidance without drawing attention to themselves.
- Make tasks manageable, with reasonable examples of what can be achieved.
- Try timed tasks, or sections of tasks.
- Set a realistic schedule.

- Keep track of how long tasks take and use this to predict future tasks more accurately.
- Keep a success log of what has been done well.
- Break tasks down.
- Practise ways to get started. Either give starting sentences for writing or ask students to keep a list of their own.
- Prioritise tasks.
- Build a "starter habit" or quick routine to help students "cue in" to work.
- Draw a black dot or line on a page showing expected length of writing.
- Give options where possible to enable low-stakes experimentation.
- Schedule fun and relaxation. Encourage all students to participate in at least one extracurricular activity at school or home and keep to it no matter what. Even in intense exam or revision time, when they might reduce some activities, they should keep something as a break.

Although many of these strategies are useful, excessive use of them can be a sign of perfectionism. So, a revision timetable that includes blocks of time for revision, school, activities and so on is a good idea. Making a detailed to-do list that includes getting up, showering and brushing hair is not.

Building resilience and courage

The word "resilience" is becoming a bit overused. In some cases, it's used as a way to throw responsibility back on to the individual: "If you can't cope with intense and difficult situations, it's because you're not resilient enough." That's not a very helpful attitude. In education, courage is when you try to do something you're not sure about. Resilience is when you learn from the experience and try something else if it goes wrong. But you have to have the chance to succeed in the first place.

As I've discussed elsewhere, the word "failure" is so loaded that it's impossible to break the barrier. And, in any case, schools simply aren't a place where it's "OK to fail". The whole system is built on a one-shot attempt at success and students know that. As teachers, we might keep the wider purpose of education in mind, but as Year 11 gets more manic, that wider purpose tends to fall by the wayside. So how about we build a culture of experimentation, not failure. When we "experiment", we know there's a chance we won't get the outcome we hoped for, but that's OK – it gives us feedback for the next time. Some experiments will teach you things. Some will teach you things you didn't expect. And some will just fizzle out.

There's been a bit of a backlash against Carol Dweck's notion of "growth mindsets", but her work casts light on perfectionists, who frequently believe they won't be able to *become* good enough either. Everyone has a combination of fixed and growth mindsets, depending on what it is they're trying to do, what aspect of their life they're thinking about, and what skills or abilities are involved. It's no good simply *telling* someone to have a growth mindset – they have to see change in action.

A culture of experimentation is not best developed in Year 11, when tensions are high and the pressure to gain good results is on. The time to experiment is before the exam: in English, for example, the creative writing section is often difficult, and students will regularly write stories that don't really work for one reason or another. They need experimentation time in Year 11 to figure more of this out. But the culture of experimentation needs to start in Year 7 and before. Offer students a choice of questions to answer – sometimes even the realisation that they should have picked the other one is valuable. Explore options when it comes to answering questions or sitting exams, to encourage consideration of what works for them and reinforce the message that not everyone works in the same way.

Give students lots of opportunities for low-stakes work. Not just low-stakes tests or quizzes, though those are immensely useful for knowledge recall and can build the confidence to have more courage in experimentation. Low-stakes *work* can include writing that is self-assessed, not read by a teacher. Paragraphs of exploratory writing. Answering exam questions not with the explicit intention to get them all right, but to find out where their gaps are. Low-stakes doesn't mean "worthless" – it means that students aren't assessed on whether they get it all right.

Self-soothing and mental fitness techniques are useful here, too. If girls are mentally strong and able to calm and soothe themselves, they're more likely to be interested in experimentation.

Extracurricular activities are critical to building resilience and courage, because they're separated from the academic, where "failure" is so much more loaded. Knitting, for example, is a great resilience builder. It's pretty hard for a novice to knit and purl, but soon, with a bit of perseverance, you've finished a whole ball of yarn and have something resembling a scarf. A bit of a wonky one, probably, with some holes from dropped stitches, but after that you have choices. Knit another ball of wool and try to get even stitches. Start a project that has more purpose. Try cable or ribbing. Try stripes. Build on a simple pattern to create something a bit more complicated. Then try a harder pattern, or three colours, or stitch two bits of knitting together.

These skills are low stakes. They can help to familiarise students with the process of learning and show them what development feels like. Novices usually progress at a quicker rate, but students have been reading and writing since they were five and so the gains are relatively small. Yet success in one aspect of their lives can carry over into others: they remember how it feels to be successful and they want more of it. Low-stakes activities are an opportunity for relaxation and enjoyment, which can reduce stress. Students can experiment with self-expression in a way that doesn't affect their academic success or failure, and thus build their confidence.

- Do pastoral and academic staff understand what perfectionism is and how to recognise the behaviours associated with it?
- Do any students regularly redo sections of work in all subjects?
- Is there a culture of editing and redrafting in the school, to encourage students to see their work as "in progress" rather than "finished"?
- Are students shown other works in progress – such as first drafts of poetry or sketches for paintings – to demonstrate the creative process and its iterations?
- Do students try different approaches to the same task, to learn that there's no perfect way?
- When scrutinising work, how much attention is paid to the look or organisation as a proxy for learning? (Some organisation is essential, but where do we draw a line?)
- Are students given the chance to experiment with their learning and sometimes keep the result private if it hasn't worked?
- Is there an extracurricular programme that gives students the opportunity to be a novice and experiment with learning in different ways?
- Are homework tasks clearly defined, both in terms of success criteria and expectations of time spent?
- Are there opportunities for low-stakes testing and low-stakes work?

FURTHER RESOURCES

Books that help younger children to see the opportunity in mistakes include
Beautiful Oops! by Barney Saltzberg and **Penelope Perfect** by Shannon
Anderson.

Ann Marie Dobosz's **The Perfectionism Workbook for Teens** is a clearly written
and well-structured set of worksheets, discussions and think pieces for
students to complete independently (but they would benefit from some
supervision, as this kind of approach tends to bring up other emotions).

"The power of vulnerability" is a compelling talk by the research professor Brené
Brown about the potential dangers of perfectionism. It's ideal for sharing with
students. *ted.com/talks/brene_brown_the_power_of_vulnerability*

Wreck This Journal by Keri Smith (and others like it) encourages users to rip, tear
and otherwise deface its pages to develop a less-than-perfect journal. Similarly,
mindful colouring books can encourage a focus on enjoyment rather than
beauty and perfection.

15. Financial literacy

A woman must have money and a room of her own if she is to write fiction – Virginia Woolf, *A Room of One's Own*

To paraphrase the psychotherapist Susie Orbach, finance is a feminist issue. Money is a difficult topic for many people and one that can even be taboo. Attitudes towards money are often deeply held and rooted in other beliefs about family, work and self-esteem.

Understanding money and how it works can be the difference between living well and barely scraping by. And although money might not buy happiness, it creates the circumstances in which happiness can thrive. This is not to say that people on low incomes can't be happy, but it's certainly easier when you're confident your mortgage will be paid and your children fed. And it can buy some measure of happiness: research shows that spending money in accordance with your goals and values, or in ways that lead to more time to spend with family and friends, can indeed result in people being less stressed, more relaxed and more joyful.[254]

When considering a feminist approach to financial education, the issues are much broader than whether men and women receive equal

---

254. Bronfenbrenner Center for Translational Research, "Can money buy happiness?", *Psychology Today*, 28 February 2019

pay. Attitudes to work, family and caring have a greater impact on women. Historically, women have been financially reliant on men, and that has developed high-pressure stereotypes about male providers and breadwinners. This, coupled with the fact that many families simply don't talk much about money, means teenagers have little idea of the cost of things, or how to budget, save or plan for the future. They don't have the opportunity to develop their own outlook on money because they don't have much information about it.

Attitudes to money remain deeply gendered. According to a study of media messages, 65% of articles define women as excessive spenders and 90% of female-targeted articles encourage women to spend less. In comparison, 70% of male-directed articles emphasise that making money is a masculine ideal and position financial success as essential to enhancing personal status. And 50% use "fear propositions to trigger actions like investing or saving, relying on masculine stereotypes and codes of combat, strength, power and competition". In magazines for men, 60% of articles assume a high level of financial literacy.[255]

Finances are another area where we've made rapid progress towards equality: until 1975, it was legal for banks to refuse mortgages without a male guarantor. But the progress is far from complete. Women are far, far less likely to invest money and their personal savings are more likely to be in a standard savings account, which suggests they're more likely to be short-term and grow less.[256]

Financial independence

Financially, women are affected more negatively when it comes to transitional life events like divorce, and women currently claim less confidence and knowledge about money than men.[257] Globally, this is

255. Anne Boden, "Why we need to #makemoneyequal", *Women Investing: what are the hurdles?*, MHP Communications, 2018

256. Helen Pankhurst, *Deeds Not Words: the story of women's rights – then and now*, Sceptre, 2018

257. "International Women's Day – the fin cap gender gap", The Money Charity, 8 March 2018

a real problem. The economic empowerment of women is associated, like female involvement in education, with better healthcare and life expectancy, economic growth and improvements in technology – and all this creates a virtuous circle.[258]

Financial independence is important for everyone, but particularly for women. Margaret Atwood's *The Handmaid's Tale* includes a scene where women are cut off from their money without warning: all funds are transferred to a man responsible for them. And because all transactions are cashless, women are rendered completely helpless and dependent. Although we might not be at risk from that particular government-led attack, domestic abuse also often includes financial control. Even in relatively amicable relationships, financial independence creates freedom. In a survey, significantly more women than men said that, for financial reasons, they were likely to stay in a relationship they wanted to leave.[259] Having your own money, and the autonomy it brings, builds self-confidence and self-belief. We don't want to indoctrinate girls with distrust when it comes to future relationships, but they should be aware of self-protection measures and encouraged to think about their attitudes and values surrounding money.

And, although retirement is the last thing teenage girls are thinking about, they need to learn to consider their financial futures, especially as there's increasing onus on the individual to improve their pension savings. By the time women reach pension age, they're more likely to be living in low-income households, with an average income of just 85% of their male counterparts.[260] But long before that, lack of savings is an issue: 15% of British people have no savings at all, with one in three saying they have less than £1500 (the general advice is to have enough money saved to support yourself for three to six months, in case of unemployment or illness).[261]

258. "Facts and figures: economic empowerment", UN Women, accessed 2019
259. Kayla Kerr, "Couples staying together because they can't afford to break up", Nutmeg, 18 February 2014
260. *Older Women in the Workplace: equal pay and pensions – women's inequality in retirement*, Close the Gap, December 2014
261. Charlie Barton, "Saving statistics", Finder, accessed 2019

Employment and money

Here in the UK, the gender pay gap still exists. In April 2019, median pay for all employees was 17.3% less for women than for men.[262] Equal pay for equal work might be the law, but it has a fairly narrow meaning. A lot of factors are at play in the pay gap, and discussing these with students makes them aware of how the choices they make (or are forced to make through social expectation) might advantage or disadvantage their earning potential. In particular, women's average pay across a company may be lower because women tend to be in lower-paid jobs and are more likely to be part-time. Statistics show that women working full-time earn 11.5% less than men working full-time, while women working part-time earn 32.4% less than men working full-time.[263] This is a social issue: women often take more time out of their careers to care for children and there's nothing wrong with this. But there is something wrong when women are *expected* to sacrifice their earning potential. Yet, as I explored in the introduction, time after time women and men experience narrow thinking when it comes to work-life balance.

Women's employment choices are affected by family responsibilities:

- Parental leave often favours women, either because men are more highly paid or because employers have discriminatory policies that haven't been updated since the introduction of shared parental leave.
- Women tend to take on more childcare responsibilities, and either work part-time or are limited in their job options because companies don't offer flexible working.
- Women taking time out have more gaps in their employment history, less relevant recent experience and miss out on pension contributions.

---

262. Brigid Francis-Devine and Doug Pyper, *The Gender Pay Gap: briefing paper number 7068*, House of Commons Library, 2 January 2020

263. *Older Women in the Workplace: equal pay and pensions – women's inequality in retirement*, Close the Gap, December 2014

Our students have to start thinking about how they want their lives to look, for family and work, and how they can challenge companies to be more creative in their employment practices.

Self-confidence and ambition

A common explanation for the pay gap is that women are less likely to negotiate their salaries.[264] And compelling recent research suggests that when women do ask, they aren't given a pay rise as often as men.[265] This study also found that "asking behaviour" was different. Older, long-tenured and full-time workers tended to ask more – those who felt more secure in their jobs to begin with. More positively, the research found that younger women asked at a similar rate to younger men, although this changed with age, seemingly as women fell out of the "full-time, experienced" category. So, while there is perhaps sexism in the workplace, leading to a higher refusal rate for women, if we give students the self-confidence to recognise their own value and worth and to logically argue for what they want, then they can fight their corner.

Another theory about women's financial potential is that they don't put themselves forward for promotion as often because they underrate their own performance, while men overrate theirs.[266] Women also seem to apply for jobs less frequently than men, but there's conflicting evidence about why. As we saw in the previous chapter, women often don't apply for jobs unless they feel they meet all the criteria, while men will on average apply if they meet 60% of the criteria. But the leadership coach Tara Mohr suggests this is not necessarily down to a lack of self-esteem; rather, women see applying as a waste of time and energy if they don't meet the criteria.[267] According to Mohr, this is because women are still more compliant and self-regulating, and they wait for others to

264. Sheryl Sandberg, *Lean In: women, work and the will to lead*, Knopf, 2013

265. Benjamin Artz, Amanda Goodall and Andrew J Oswald, "Research: women ask for raises as often as men, but are less likely to get them", *Harvard Business Review*, 25 June 2018

266. Jan Hills and Francesca Hills, *Brain-Savvy Woman: how women can overcome gender bias and succeed at work*, Head Heart + Brain, 2017

267. Tara Mohr, *Playing Big: a practical guide for brilliant women like you*, Arrow, 2015

notice their value rather than pushing themselves forward. Although we value those skills in academic life and exam achievement, they do women a disservice in the workplace. If women were promoted at the same rate as men (they're approximately 18% less likely) then the number of women in leadership positions would double.[268] It's not necessarily women's self-confidence that holds them back, but we need to foster confidence in students so that they keep putting themselves forward and keep pushing at the glass ceiling.

Investments are another area of finance where women's risk-aversion might be holding them back. Research suggests women see the stock market as basically gambling, but don't fully understand the financial sector.[269] The majority of women avoid high-risk strategies or don't manage their money much at all, and end up by default in low-risk, low-return investments; 52% of women prefer lower-risk despite knowing they will receive less in the long term, compared with 36% of men.[270]

"Being ambitious" is still something that women are encouraged to avoid – at least openly. Perhaps one of the first steps in success, financial or personal, is simply admitting what you want out loud to yourself and others. Being open about your ambition is critical and helps others around you to be ambitious, too.[271] As teachers, we can openly acknowledge and encourage ambition in our students, in part by enlisting external speakers or considering the contact students have with working people. Ask guest speakers to talk about money and salaries, as well as their future ambitions.

It's fine if a girl's ambition isn't to be chief executive of her own company by 30, or to be foreign secretary. But both these ambitions have been expressed by girls in lessons of mine and some other students laughed. That disbelief could be really damaging to a student's

268. Jan Hills and Francesca Hills, *Brain-Savvy Woman: how women can overcome gender bias and succeed at work*, Head Heart + Brain, 2017

269. Claer Barrett, "Even women who can handle money are reluctant investors", *Financial Times*, 8 March 2018

270. *Women Investing: what are the hurdles?*, MHP Communications, 2018

271. Jennifer O'Connell, "Ambition: why is it still a dirty word for women?", *The Irish Times*, 20 October 2018

confidence, but it also reveals the perceived absurdity of girls standing up and saying what they want to achieve. We encourage goal- and target-setting in schools, but do we really look beyond grades to where girls' achievements can take them?

The aim of becoming "wealthy" is frequently subject to inverse snobbery. Everyone has their own level of financial ambition: for some, it's to be comfortably able to pay the mortgage and an unexpected car repair bill without dipping into debt. For others, it's to earn enough to be able to become a philanthropist.[272] There are moral questions about wealth distribution, but students should be encouraged to question and determine their own values surrounding money, and how they can blend their home and work lives successfully.

What should we teach?

We can't teach students everything they need to know about finance and investment. But we can foster the skills they need to be able to explore, understand and evaluate the options available to them. Focus on the basics:

- Regular saving – "paying yourself first".
- Budgeting, including saving for the short and long term.
- What a payslip looks like and what the deductions pay for. This is also a chance to explore the idea of wealth creation and philanthropy – social responsibility starts with understanding taxes.
- Financial vocabulary.
- Compound interest – its dangers in debt and benefits in savings.

Even people who don't like discussing their own money love discussing other people's! Money diaries can be an interesting way for students to explore their own attitudes and values – the website Refinery29, for example, publishes a weekly money diary by a female contributor that gives their age, salary and situation, then tracks their weekly spend (be

272. Stephanie Shirley, "Why do ambitious women have flat heads?" (talk), ted.com, March 2015

careful to keep any discussion judgement-free!). Consideration of the variety of choices that people make – whether they spend a fortune on make-up, invest for the future or work freelance on a low wage – helps students to become confident in talking about money and their financial priorities.

- Can we invite entrepreneurial speakers to discuss their day-to-day activities with students and engage in an open Q&A?
- Do our students talk about their financial aspirations? Can they break savings goals down and understand how compound interest can help them?
- Are teachers confident in delivering financial literacy, using the appropriate vocabulary?
- Is conversation about ambition and money gender-neutral?
- Can students explore their values and attitudes towards money, including how money might play into ideas about self-esteem, family roles and responsibilities, and identity?
- Do students have the chance to explore their ambitions regarding home/family life, and consider the impact their choices could have?
- Do they have opportunities to discuss how to challenge this when the impact might be based on sexism?

FURTHER RESOURCES

Make £5 Grow is a programme available to primaries but the resources are free for all to access. Each student team is given £5 and a time frame to make as much money as they can. *make-5-grow.co.uk*

The Money Charity offers advice and information on financial products, debt and student finances. *themoneycharity.org.uk*

The Student Investor Challenge helps students to explore how the stock market works, tasking them to work in teams to develop a (virtual) stock portfolio. *studentinvestor.org*

Young Enterprise provides resources and guidance on financial literacy and enterprise education. It runs the Young Enterprise competition nationally, in which students develop and run a small company, gaining business skills as well as financial literacy. *young-enterprise.org.uk*

Young Money has produced a free downloadable textbook on financial matters aimed at students aged 14–16. *tinyurl.com/u9ywtav*

Part IV
Modelling the feminist society

Taught from their infancy that beauty is woman's
sceptre, the mind shapes itself to the body, and roaming
round its gilt cage, only seeks to adorn its prison –
Mary Wollstonecraft, *A Vindication of the Rights of Woman*

We still think of a powerful man as a born leader and
a powerful woman as an anomaly – **Margaret Atwood**

Schools are a fascinating microcosm of their wider communities. We have an awesome power to be able to model to students the values for their adult lives – and this includes modelling the feminist society we wish them to inhabit. A society that values women and men equally. A society that interrogates thinking around gender, carefully considers it, and decides whether to challenge or uphold its representation.

In the introduction, I talked about the traditional "masculine" and "feminine" characteristics and working towards the agreement that all men and women possess a blend of both. In Part IV, I'm going to look at the ways in which schools can model a more feminist society to students, by bringing these qualities into our day-to-day practice and by modelling a feminist approach to work. An awful lot of social input goes into creating people's concepts of gender and children are getting this input all the time from all angles. It can seem a Sisyphean task to tackle those messages. But young people spend an awful lot of time in school, and if we can explicitly counteract some of the implicit messages they receive elsewhere, it's a really great start.

16. Feminist leadership

For the master's tools will never dismantle the master's house. They may allow us to temporarily beat him at his own game, but they will never enable us to bring about genuine change – Audre Lorde

It's clear from the numbers that there are barriers to women becoming leaders in teaching. Teaching is a female-dominated profession but with male-dominated leadership. Across the profession, 74% of classroom teachers are female (90% in primary schools!) but 66% of headteachers are female. At secondary, it's 64% of classroom teachers and just 39% of headteachers.[273] Statistics aren't readily available for support staff, but in many schools the gender pay gap is substantial: one report suggests that 40 of the 100 companies with the biggest pay gaps in England, Wales and Scotland are schools.[274] This seems likely to be related to the factors I discussed in Part III. Women are more likely to work part-time, they're less likely to take on leadership positions, and the lower-paid support

---

273. Valentine Mulholland, "Why are there disproportionately few female school leaders and why are they paid less than their male colleagues?", *TES*, 8 March 2018, and Nicky Morgan, speech at Empowering Women in Education Leadership Conference, 18 March 2015

274. Branwen Jeffreys, "Why do schools have a massive pay gap?", BBC News, 20 March 2018

staff are more likely to be women. The National Education Union also reports that the gender pay gap as a whole is lower among classroom teachers (with women earning £900 less than men) but widens the higher up the responsibility ladder you go: female headteachers in state-funded education earn, on average, £5,700 less than their male counterparts.[275]

What are the barriers?

In many cases, the barriers faced by women in teaching are the same as in many other professions:

- Unconscious bias in hiring practices, either through language choices in recruitment adverts or a belief that a more masculine leadership style is preferable and more effective.
- Bias against women in leadership.
- Workload expectations leading to difficulty in achieving work-life balance.

It's easy to read this and think something along the lines of: women need to get over it; they need to put aside their concerns about work-life balance and just join the race if they want to win it. But that argument ignores the fact that such competitive and blinkered approaches to leadership, to any job, can't be feminist because they sideline women's concerns and overlook the very real social pressures that they are often juggling. Such an argument maintains a polarised masculine approach, which inevitably places "being masculine" in the same category as "being in charge".

Let's explore those barriers faced by women in depth.

1. Unconscious bias in hiring practices

Think about your school's recruitment process when hiring staff at all levels. Are there opportunities for applicants to demonstrate their personal approaches and styles, which will show the difference they can

---

275. "Gender pay gap", National Education Union, 20 December 2018

make to the school? General questions about leadership aren't likely to elicit the same richness of response as asking about their own values and potential. Everything from interview panels to the questions asked can potentially send gender-biased signals: have several people looked at these and discussed them in detail?

Job adverts for school leaders often reflect gender bias, portraying a school as a particularly "masculine" or "feminine" workplace and limiting the diversity of applicants.[276] Vivienne Porritt, co-founder of #WomenEd, has argued that words like "driven" and "ambitious" describe, however unconsciously, a masculine leadership style that puts the individual front and centre as "dynamic", "authoritative" and "challenging".[277] These aren't the words women usually use to describe themselves, even if they might be those things. Such words suggest a job that will require more than they can give while maintaining their work-life balance and juggling all society's other demands. For many women, these adverts suggest a 24/7 approach to work that is simply unsustainable.

Such descriptions can often be seen throughout a school's statements of ethos, vision and values, and represent the school in a gendered way. As I discussed in the introduction, gender stereotypes exist and it's not necessarily their existence that is problematic, but their polarity and the fact that they are applied to the sexes wholesale. When this binary is applied to adverts for leadership, we need to think about the message we are sending about who and what values are wanted for the position.

2. Bias against female leaders
When women *are* recruited to leadership positions, it's an unhappy truth that they are often viewed with suspicion, even by other women. More than men, female leaders have a difficult line to walk. Too authoritative and they are perceived as bitchy, arrogant and cold – all code, really, for

---

276. Danielle Gaucher, Justin Friesen and Aaron C Kay, "Evidence that gendered wording in job advertisements exists and sustains gender inequality", *Journal of Personality and Social Psychology*, 101:1, 2011

277. Louise Tickle, "Language in school job ads puts women off headteacher roles", *The Guardian*, 19 June 2018

"unfeminine". Too warm and they're seen as "soft" and not tough enough to get the job done.[278] Studies have examined the words that are coded as stereotypically masculine and feminine:

Masculine	Feminine
Active	Committed
Ambition	Compassionate
Assert	Cooperative
Challenge	Honest
Confident	Interpersonal
Courageous	Loyal
Decisive	Kind
Principle	Responsive
Self-sufficient	Sensitive
Self-reliant	Supportive
	Warm

Again, the problem isn't necessarily the stereotyping of two types of being. The problem is aligning one type to "better" leadership and not acknowledging that a blend of the two is probably ideal. Truly great leaders draw on qualities from both lists to solve the different problems they face.

3. Workload

The 2019 Teacher Wellbeing Index shows that 68% of senior leaders work more than 51 hours a week and 84% describe themselves as stressed.[279] The survey suggests that most teachers are struggling to some extent with their workload, work-life balance and ability to switch off: 71% of education professionals cited workload as the main reason for considering leaving their jobs, while 78% have experienced behavioural, psychological or physical symptoms due to their work. This is not an acceptable level of stress for either sex and we need to move faster to address it.

Workload is a feminist issue and it has a disproportionate impact on women aged 30–39, who make up 23% of the profession but 27% of

278. *Women 'Take Care', Men 'Take Charge': stereotyping of US business leaders exposed*, Catalyst, 2005

279. *Teacher Wellbeing Index 2019*, Education Support

the leavers. A Policy Exchange report[280] suggested that because some of these teachers return to the profession later, it seems likely that this age group is struggling most to reconcile the demands of family and career. Around half of those who leave the profession for family reasons seem to return, but by that point they are less experienced (with less up-to-date curriculum knowledge, which might hamper their chances of promotion) and less financially secure.

What is feminist leadership?

Feminist leadership has characteristics associated with the social constructs of femininity: cooperation, nurture, intuition. It focuses on consensus-building, creativity and kindness. Women tend towards this more collaborative, less individualistic style of leadership.[281]

Feminist leadership is also authentic: women and men are enabled to lead in whatever style best suits them and their organisation, without worrying about fitting into a particular mould, gendered or otherwise.[282] Collaborative leadership doesn't work in all situations all the time – there are always moments that require an authoritative decision or a firm hand. But for the majority of the time, a feminist workplace that values cooperation, collaboration and nurture will extend those values to its staff. In almost any industry, results will improve dramatically, because such workplaces encourage greater creativity and commitment from staff, who feel they belong.[283] In these workplaces, everyone – male and female – can flourish and deliver their individual best in their own way.

The television show *The Apprentice* has a lot to answer for and reflects an old-fashioned "alpha male" style of individual leadership. Its contestants

280. Jonathan Simons, "Let's talk about flex" in *The Importance of Teachers: a collection of essays on teacher recruitment and retention*, ed. Jonathan Simons, Policy Exchange, 2016

281. Peter J Kuhn and Marie-Claire Villeval, "Are women more attracted to cooperation than men?", *The Economic Journal*, 125:582, February 2015

282. Alice H Eagly and Mary C Johannesen-Schmidt, "The leadership styles of women and men", *Journal of Social Issues*, 57:4, January 2001

283. Juliet Bourke and Bernadette Dillon, "The diversity and inclusion revolution: eight powerful truths", *Deloitte Review*, issue 22, January 2018

are usually arrogant, obnoxious, convinced of their own value, and take every opportunity to promote their own achievements while subtly or openly denigrating others. This toxic approach to business management rewards selfish and damaging behaviour. Thankfully, this style isn't seen often in schools, but there is a tendency to see leaders as individual visionaries. Many educational leadership programmes discuss the need for a leader to be personally inspiring, drive the vision forward, and approach change management through what sometimes amounts to a cult of personality.

Clearly, we want leaders to have expertise and purpose. Without those qualities, it's very difficult for them to take the organisation anywhere. But a leadership style that's more individual than inclusive is risky for the long-term wellbeing of a company. In his book *Good to Great*, Jim Collins explores business leadership in different industries and identifies the factors that help some organisations to succeed while others flounder. Without exception, the more successful companies were those with collaborative and distributed leadership: a more feminine model.[284] The most important quality for leaders? Humility. The capacity to say, "It's not about me, it's about us." The ability to find a balance between taking their due credit and celebrating everyone else's contributions. Feminist leadership isn't about being falsely modest, or so self-effacing that you're barely there. Rather, it's about being able to confidently acknowledge what you have brought to the table and what everyone else has brought, too.

In an article for *The New York Times*, Tina Brown presents an interesting take on why women such as Jacinda Ardern, the prime minister of New Zealand, and Nancy Pelosi, speaker of the US House of Representatives, are so successful:

> *"The alchemy of what has made women the way they are is mysterious: Is it a result of centuries spent trying to survive and prosper in societies where they've been viewed as lesser? Or, until recently, of always being appointed the family caregiver, bearing and raising children, tending*

---

284. Jim Collins, *Good to Great*, Random House, 2001

to elderly parents and disabled siblings, so often left to shoulder the unpaid burdens of real life? Women have learned and taught lessons about how to cope with seeming impossibilities in ways that men traditionally – and to this day – have not. Coaching a slow learner on homework after a day of hassles at the office provides a deep experience of delayed gratification. A woman's wisdom comes, in part, from the great juggle of her life."[285]

The ability to balance the responsibilities of family and work, which has been passed down through generations of women, cultivates a different kind of wisdom and a different kind of role model. Men need the chance to gain this wisdom and experience, and that is an equally important reason to gain equality for women in the workplace. Men need to know that they don't have to rush to participate in a purely masculine way of leading, and they don't have to leave their innate feminine qualities at home.

One of the most confident things a leader can do is to rank their contribution as equal to that of others, without worrying about shoring up their status or position. It's enough that you have the leadership position and have led the team; you don't need the external validation of others. Have the self-possession to congratulate others and be genuinely happy for their success. For me, this humble leadership is encapsulated in the public eye by Barack and Michelle Obama. Both appear completely confident in their own position; they are never arrogant or self-aggrandising, but generous in their praise of others.

Leadership at all levels

Leadership needs to be as evenly distributed as possible at all levels and in all skill sets. Obviously, there are challenges in creating equality. I wouldn't for a second suggest quotas, for example, as I firmly believe the best person needs to get the job. But, too often, unconscious bias is making the decisions.

---

285. Tina Brown, "What happens when women stop leading like men", *The New York Times*, 30 March 2019

When we look at the leadership in a school, do we see gender bias at work? Are there more women leading in pastoral and SEND roles (the more "nurturing" areas) than in data, timetabling and curriculum?[286] What is the balance like in different departments, faculties and across the senior leadership team?

Much of this imbalance can, as with workload, have to do with expectations in the workplace and the way that senior and middle leaders represent their working lives to those around them. If they're constantly pressured, stressed and harassed, then the message comes across even more strongly to women that this job is not for them – at least, not if they want to have a family as well. Men are sent the opposite message: this is for you, as long as you've got someone to watch the kids.

But leadership is an opportunity to do things differently. Leaders have lighter timetables and can be more flexible: using their PPA time to visit their child's primary school, for example, sends a strong message that empowers others lower down the hierarchy to ask for such things themselves. Personally, I'm strongly in favour of that kind of compassionate workplace, and I believe all policies should be available equitably. But there's something very powerful about actually *seeing* senior leaders leave at 4pm, rather than simply being told on paper that the option is there but never witnessing anyone do it. Better balance is better for everybody.

Growing leaders

Leadership doesn't have to involve membership of the SLT. Many teachers feel more empowered and autonomous when they're given an opportunity to lead something meaningful in their school, no matter how small it might appear. There's absolutely nothing wrong with wanting to be "just" a classroom teacher, but if people are interested, we must offer them chances to lead from early in their careers:

---

286. Claire Nicholls, "Removing the blinkers" in *10% Braver: inspiring women to lead education*, eds. Vivienne Porritt and Keziah Featherstone, Sage, 2019

- Provide opportunities to act up or shadow leaders for extended periods of time, so they understand the realities and experiences of leadership.
- Use TLR3 positions strategically to add leadership capacity for projects and develop teachers' expertise in different subjects or whole-school.
- Establish meaningful professional development in which staff lead CPD in areas where they have expertise and confidence.
- Distribute leadership among staff – for example, sharing assemblies, revision planning, mentoring student teachers or undertaking small whole-school projects for a fixed term.

Part-time leadership

There is a worrying perception that leaders can't be part-time. A National Foundation for Educational Research study cited school leaders who said they would not let middle or senior leaders work part-time because "they thought it would make it impossible to undertake strategic duties, manage staff and lead teams effectively".[287] This is a barrier faced disproportionately by women, as they're more likely to want to be part-time. Yet there are plenty of leaders at all levels who work part-time, job-share or have flexible working arrangements: it can be done. Timetables can be adapted to ensure there are always enough leaders on-site. Communication is essential in all directions, but if both employee and employer are willing to discuss and compromise, solutions can be found that suit everyone. It's much better to retain a good teacher some of the time than to lose them completely.

---

287. Caroline Sharp, Robert Smith, Jack Worth and Jens Van den Brande, *Part-Time Teaching and Flexible Working in Secondary Schools*, National Foundation for Educational Research, June 2019

- Do we have a broad gender balance in leadership across the school and across subjects?
- Do we track applicants' genders to ensure we get a balanced field of candidates?
- Have we checked our adverts for unconscious gender bias?[288]
- Have we examined our recruitment practice from advert to interview, to ensure assessment is free of gender bias?
- Are leaders and governors/trustees aware of unconscious bias issues?
- Do views on leadership in the school allow for a range of approaches?
- Do teaching staff have opportunities to act up, lead projects, shadow senior leaders and work with those above them, in order to develop their leadership skills and confidence?
- Has any pay gap in the school been investigated to understand its origins?
- As leaders, male and female, have we considered what blend of masculine and feminine qualities works for us and our contexts?

288. Totaljobs has developed an online tool to help: totaljobs.com/insidejob/gender-bias-decoder

FURTHER RESOURCES

10% Braver: Inspiring Women to Lead Education (edited by Vivienne Porritt and
Keziah Featherstone) contains case studies and personal accounts from female
leaders across the education sector, exploring topics like flexible working,
gendered barriers and impostor syndrome.

The Equality and Diversity Fund from the Department for Education supports
projects to improve diversity in school leadership. Its website includes
information on how to apply for funding. *gov.uk/guidance/equality-and-
diversity-funding-for-school-led-projects*

#WomenEd offers resources and events to support women to reach their
leadership potential. *womened.org*

The government's **Women Leading in Education** regional networks organise
conferences, training and discussions on developing women's leadership
potential. *gov.uk/guidance/women-leading-in-education-regional-networks*

The Women's Resource Centre runs its feminist leadership training programme in
locations around the UK. *wrc.org.uk*

17. Family-friendly working

We think, mistakenly, that success is the result of the amount of time we put in at work, instead of the quality of time we put in – **Arianna Huffington, *Thrive***

As I said in Part III, feminist workplaces have an important role to play in the long game of social change. As long as family caring expectations continue to fall on women, they will be only able to fully participate in work if it doesn't take over their life. And men will only be able to play a full and vibrant role at home when they aren't expected to give their lives to their work.

A sustainable work environment supports all staff. There's no doubt that the statistics on teacher stress in the previous chapter show that, for many, working in this profession is completely unsustainable – and women are disproportionately affected. When it comes to family responsibilities, women's salaries are often expected to cover childcare costs, so they need a pretty big incentive to come to work when only a fraction of their pay is left afterwards. Sometimes, though, there's not even a fraction left. Rebecca Foster, an associate senior leader and head of English, wrote a blog in 2015 in which she described herself as "paying to teach"; with two children in nursery, her salary didn't cover their childcare fees.[289] Rebecca made this choice because she values her identity as a teacher and wanted to ensure her continuing experience in the profession – she brims with enthusiasm for her job and her workplace.

The MaternityTeacher PaternityTeacher Project, founded by Emma Sheppard, collated statistics that demonstrate why schools need to be "life-friendly":

- 60% of female headteachers are parents, compared with 90% of male headteachers.
- More than half of teachers have children under 18.
- An average of two women per school are on maternity leave at any given time.
- More than half of teachers leaving to look after families don't return to the classroom.[290]

A lack of support for women in the workplace can harm their careers. It can also lead to a dearth of female role models in classrooms at a time when young people are looking around them to see how adults manage their lives. If we want more feminist, equal relationships and caring arrangements in the future, we need to model them.

There's no doubt that pupils do better, pastorally and academically, when staff are productive, happy and well looked after. High morale leads to lower staff turnover, less absence, less supply cover and vacancies that can be filled more easily. In turn, this not only means schools have more cash to spend in other areas, but also that staff are able to build better relationships over time, and to get into their teaching rhythm rather than emotionally fire-fighting and constantly considering whether to stay or go.[291]

Ofsted has started drawing attention to the issue of workload, and included this evaluation criterion in the "leadership and management" section of the 2019 inspection framework:

289. Rebecca Foster, "On why I pay to teach", thelearningprofession.com (blog), 22 May 2015
290. "Research", mtpt.org.uk, accessed 2019
291. *Teacher Wellbeing Index 2019*, Education Support

"Leaders engage with their staff and are aware and take account of the main pressures on them. They are realistic and constructive in the way that they manage staff, including their workload."[292]

Anyone who addresses workload simply to meet Ofsted criteria likely won't be successful, but this is a sign of the issue moving up the agenda – and it's about time. The problem has to be approached from a position of genuinely wanting staff to be motivated, fulfilled and happy to come to work.

Staff satisfaction

Schools are really interesting places when it comes to employee/customer models. Schools don't much like to consider themselves as businesses; it can feel as if this undermines the moral and social vocation of teaching, and that a business approach is somehow ruthless and capitalistic, associated with profit. Yet the most successful businesses are often the ones that prioritise the happiness and wellbeing of their staff.[293] The immediate difficulty here for schools is that we always put the students first. I think we need to think a bit differently about it.

The measures of success for a school might be student achievement and their wider wellbeing, but those successes are more likely to come if we focus on our staff in a positive, productive and supportive way. The best businesses also reward staff based on *what they do* rather than on outcomes alone. If schools use performance-related pay based on student data, this is problematic, because teachers lack control over the outcome: the data is affected by the students themselves, their attitudes and home lives, the previous four teachers they had in the subject, and so many other factors.

Jason Whitman, vice-president of employee success at Justworks, has suggested the following areas as part of a positive focus on staff:[294]

---

292. *The Education Inspection Framework*, Ofsted, May 2019

293. Andrew Chamberlain and Daniel Zhao, "The key to happy customers? Happy employees", *Harvard Business Review*, 19 August 2019

294. Shep Hyken, "How happy employees make happy customers", *Forbes*, 27 May 2017

- **Meaningful employee development**. This doesn't have to mean leadership roles: staff can be offered other advancement opportunities or projects that are linked with teaching and learning or pastoral initiatives. Give staff the opportunity to work with different colleagues, form different relationships with students and become more deeply involved in the school. Conversations about development should happen regularly, not just once a year in a performance management review, and can often be relatively informal.

- **Make training part of the culture**. Rather than being "one size fits all", CPD should address *need* (we wouldn't accept a lesson that didn't differentiate at all, so why do we accept CPD like this?). Whether it's in pedagogy, skills or subject knowledge, learning should be facilitated and praised for all staff, teaching and support.

- **Show employees they are supported**. This includes everything from a robust and consistent behaviour management policy that's always followed through to making the effort to check in if you know they've had a bad day. A healthy, caring and supportive environment makes everyone feel more relaxed and able to give their best.

- **Create a fun work environment**. Teaching is a strange profession because we don't work much with other adults. Create opportunities for staff to get together informally, whether it's cake at break on a Friday or a regular staff drink after school (even in the staffroom if people have to rush off quickly). Make sure whole-staff meetings aren't just a list of information without much human interaction. Teachers need spaces where they can be with each other, share ideas and let off steam.

- **Give rewards and recognition**. Say thank you. Contribute to a staff Christmas party. Buy biscuits. It's amazing how much a bit of recognition can brighten someone's day, especially in a job where teachers are so often hidden away in their own rooms. Recognition has to feel genuine, and it's no good leaving a pile of doughnuts in the staffroom if you've just added three parents' evenings to the annual calendar! Don't wait for the end of term or the year – make it a regular practice to thank staff for their specific contributions.

The workload problem

Without a robust understanding of staff workload and how leadership decisions affect it, all the recognition in the world won't make teachers' jobs sustainable. Teaching staff and leaders all have a responsibility to tackle workload. Leaders need to critically evaluate their requirements of staff and understand the pressures at different times of the year; teachers can try to find ways to work smarter and let go of some traditional expectations that are taking a toll.

In any project – like teaching a year group or subject – there are three primary forces at play:

When a project is floundering, it either needs additional time, additional funding or a reduction in quality. In teaching, we're hardly ever willing to accept a reduction in quality, because that would directly affect the grades and life chances of our students. And with cuts to school budgets, our only option has been to increase time – our time. We don't have more teachers, but our teachers are putting in more hours.

This has to stop. In a feminist model of education, it's essential that staff have a reasonable work-life balance. A society that values family, nurturing and community simply cannot allow its members to work at an unsustainable pace. If teachers burn out and cannot look after themselves (never mind others), schools become toxic workplaces where presenteeism is more important than quality of work and is taken as a marker of ability.

Sometimes, school leaders need to be courageous enough to stop doing something good in order to do something better. A strong awareness of how staff workload changes across the key stages is really important. Workload is either essential, desirable or personal.

Essential might be:
- An attainment data drop three times a year.
- Attendance data report once a month.
- Students demonstrating improvement in oral and written work.
- Shared key assessment points in the departmental scheme of work.

Desirable might be:
- A bank of revision resources on the VLE.
- Keyword displays in the corridors.

Personal might be:
- Wanting to write comments on a student's work.
- Wanting to run a lunchtime club.
- Wanting to plan lessons responsively.

Some of the personal points are habits, developed over years of teaching, or can come from a lack of confidence or an outdated belief in "what Ofsted and SLT want". Some teachers don't want to give up written marking. Some want to run three clubs a week. Those are personal choices. But if we clearly define the essential and desirable points for our contexts, then individuals will have more control over how their personal choices affect their work-life balance. The essentials should also be checked periodically, for additions that need making or points that have outstayed their welcome. If the essentials list is under control, then the desirable is achievable over time.

And the gender connection to all this? Time. And capacity. Sometimes it's easy to join the conversations of the time-poor, complaining about running three clubs a week and having to make pretty PowerPoints for every lesson, plus new board displays every few days. But these don't necessarily contribute to better teaching, and if the time input isn't outweighed by the value to students, we should direct our energy elsewhere. Perhaps into a personal hobby that is fulfilling and recharges our batteries, so we're better teachers when we're in the classroom.

Gaining control over workload creates a model of teaching and leadership that promotes the profession as manageable and enjoyable, rather than a time-sucking nightmare that steals your life for six weeks at a time. Modelling this to students is important, not just for the teaching profession, but because by engaging in discussions about how we make the workplace work for us, we help them to consider the work-life balance they want in the future.

How to tame your workload

Marking

Many schools are embracing a "what works" approach to feedback, empowering teachers to use whatever method best suits the class and the lesson. For me, the best marking method is whatever consolidates students' skills and helps them to move on to the next stage. Here are some common methods:

- Whole-class feedback.
- Verbal discussion with students or small groups.
- Live marking (in-class feedback).
- Audio recordings.
- Codes.
- Peer- and self-assessment that is scaffolded and specific.
- Guided self-assessment, including editing and review.
- Written feedback, either individual comments or whole-class.

Lesson planning

Share resources and embrace Litdrive,[295] or whatever subject-specific alternative exists (if there isn't one, collaborate to create one!). Responsive planning doesn't mean rewriting every lesson. Sometimes it's about changing the order of things, or slowing down, or taking 10 minutes to teach a list of keywords at the beginning of a lesson.

I love planning. I think it's the most creative part of teaching. I enjoy going back to a text or topic, and working out what I'm going to focus on and how I'll adapt what I've done before. For many teachers, planning is a great part of the job and removing it can take away substantial joy. It's about finding what works for you, but if planning is a *personal* rather than an *essential* then, sometimes, it needs to change.

Data collection

Schools are incredibly data-rich places, but how much of it is actually used effectively? Being judicious about what we collect and using it more effectively is the key. Always know who data is for and what its purpose is. Who's going to see it? Who's going to discuss it, analyse it, change their practice because of it? Good classroom teachers already know the data. They know who could work harder, who doesn't yet understand expanded brackets and who needs to remember to use subject vocabulary. Here are some smarter ways to use data:

- **Automate data where possible** (e.g. colour-coding, repeat information). SIMS and other data-management programs can give very quick, clear reports – it's worth taking the time to learn to use them properly. Make sure they are well maintained, by deleting reports that are no longer used, for example, so everyone can find the most up-to-date information.
- **Keep reports simple** so targets can be easily constructed and monitored.
- **Review data collection regularly**: has the purpose changed? Is it

---

295. litdrive.org.uk

being used in the same way? Is it effective? Is it single-use data or repeated? For example, if we're collecting Year 11 predictions in January, we should probably also collect them in May and August to learn how to make them more accurate, or the year after to see if our cohort is on the same track.

Administration and organisation

- **Try centrally administered and monitored detention systems** to reduce the burden on individual teachers.
- **Ensure meetings always have an agenda.** Reading materials distributed in advance will make them more decision-focused.
- **Keep meetings to time**, no matter what.

Productivity hacks

- **Save template letters and emails** in the drafts folder so you can just pull them out, rather than retyping them every time.
- **Get a good electronic filing system** and name every file properly! It makes such a difference.
- **Batch-complete tasks.** Whether it's planning, admin or marking, getting one set of tasks done is much more productive than moving back and forth. This also goes for breaking down tasks: planning five Year 10 lessons in a row is much easier than planning two, then two Year 9 lessons, then two more for Year 10.
- **Allocate PPA time to specific tasks** and book it into your diary. Figure out what is "deep work" that requires quiet and focused thinking, and "light work" that requires less concentration. Choose a time and place suited to each. I often do light work in the staffroom (emails, admin, updating my mark book, photocopying) so I can also check in with colleagues, but deep work in my classroom. Even if you don't have allocated spaces, try to find "your space". Hidden corners in the library work especially well!
- Plenty more has been written on the subject of workload, but

the following have been very useful to me: Jamie Thom, *Slow Teaching*; Kat Howard, *Stop Talking About Wellbeing*; Jennifer Webb, *How to Teach English Literature*; Alex Quigley, *The Confident Teacher*.

Flexible working

A further piece in the model-workplace puzzle is flexible working, something that schools should be able to do really well, given the piecemeal nature of our timetabled day, yet can't seem to get right.

To create a feminist working environment that supports men and women to play a full part in their home lives, whatever they involve, flexible working has to be a factor. Not an add-on, or a bonus available to senior leaders because of their reduced teaching time, or a "favour" to new parents, but a genuine reality. Some schools really struggle with this, but plenty are doing an absolutely storming job of supporting their teachers in living their lives.

The Department for Education says it believes flexible working can help to achieve gender equality in schools by:

> *"...allowing women to return to teaching on a flexible basis (for example after having children); improving the career progressions of women by offering more flexible opportunities at senior levels within the school system."*[296]

Childcare is the most common reason for flexible working requests, with work-life balance a close second.[297] A DfE report from 2013 acknowledges that there are challenges – including concerns about increased costs, managing timetables and parental expectations – but also notes that these can be overcome. It's interesting that even though it's not common to be offered or made aware of a flexible working policy,

296. "Increasing flexible working opportunities in schools", Department for Education, 11 December 2017

297. CooperGibson Research, *Exploring Flexible Working Practice in Schools: literature review*, Department for Education, January 2019

it's even less common for men: just 23% of male teachers returning from paternity leave were made aware of their right to request flexible working – another indicator that we see women as the primary carer by default.

It's also the case that 88% of senior leaders said they didn't have flexible working arrangements in their school because *staff hadn't asked*. Research from the National Foundation for Educational Research indicates that teachers thought if they *did* ask, their request wouldn't be accepted, although senior leaders responding to the same survey said they would try to accommodate it.[298] There's a clear mismatch between how teachers and leaders perceive this policy. Only by talking about flexible working and how to make it function will staff at all levels feel confident about it. And the more it's put in place, the better we'll get at managing it.

Many schools are getting flexible working right with strategies that don't simply rely on teachers going part-time:

- Autonomous use of PPA, not necessarily on-site.
- Family-friendly leave policies, including scope to attend children's plays or elderly parents' medical appointments.
- Leave allowance that staff can request as in any other job.
- Overlapping PPA for job-sharers.
- Regular meetings that are timetabled like lessons, if required.
- Different start and finish times – for example, to enable parents to do the school run but also provide end-of-the-day revision support.
- Time in lieu for overnight trips or attending parents' evenings on days off.

Research consistently suggests that the more autonomy someone has in their work, the happier they are.[299] Autonomy can come from

298. Caroline Sharp, Robert Smith, Jack Worth and Jens Van den Brande, *Part-Time Teaching and Flexible Working in Secondary Schools*, National Foundation for Educational Research, June 2019

299. Daniel Wheatley, "Autonomy in paid work and employee subjective well-being", *Work and Occupations*, 44:3, 2017

some flexible working. It can also come from enabling teachers to have creative freedom in the classroom – which, happily, can reduce workload. A double win.

- Do we have a workload policy that covers how to assess the impact of additional initiatives?
- Are there easy, non-judgemental ways for staff to convey their concerns about workload and ask for support?
- Have we aligned calendars (e.g. events, assessment, data) to ensure an even balance?
- Have we assessed the workload across the year and made accommodations at particularly busy times?
- Are workload-related policies (e.g. data, assessment) regularly reviewed and considered alongside one another?
- Is data collected for a defined purpose and used afterwards?
- Are staff encouraged to use and share methods to cut their workload and speed up admin tasks?
- Are staff engaged in meaningful CPD?
- Is CPD personalised and purposeful?
- Is CPD assessed for impact, and embedded rather than delivered as "one-off" sessions?
- How is staff morale maintained at difficult points of the year?
- Are staff, female and male, made aware of their flexible working rights?
- Are staff confident in the process for requesting flexible working?

FURTHER RESOURCES

The Department for Education's **Exploring Flexible Working Practice in Schools** report offers examples and case studies of flexible working solutions, as well as exploring some of the barriers. *tinyurl.com/v299kta*

The MaternityTeacher PaternityTeacher Project works with parents to support their transition back to work, both during parental leave and afterwards. The project also works with school leaders to explore family-friendly working practices. *mtpt.org.uk*

The government's **school workload reduction toolkit** has audits, sample policies and suggestions for reducing workload in a variety of areas, for classroom teachers and school leaders. *tinyurl.com/yenqpj9p*

Twitter is a great subject-specific resource, and there are other subject-related sharing platforms where teachers share resources, ideas and planning assets. For English teachers in particular, **Litdrive** offers a wealth of resources. *litdrive.org.uk*

Conclusion:
what happens next?

Visionary feminism is a wise and loving politics. It is rooted in the love of male and female being, refusing to privilege one over the other. The soul of feminist politics is the commitment to ending patriarchal domination of women and men, girls and boys. Love cannot exist in any relationship that is based on domination and coercion. Males cannot love themselves in patriarchal culture if their very self-definition relies on submission to patriarchal rules. When men embrace feminist thinking and practice, which emphasizes the value of mutual growth and self-actualization in all relationships, their emotional well-being will be enhanced. A genuine feminist politics always brings us from bondage to freedom, from lovelessness to loving – **bell hooks**

On some days, it can seem like genuine gender equality is very far away. Writing the final chapters of this book in the run-up to Christmas, with toy catalogues and gift guides everywhere, there are daily reminders of the work yet to do. More horrifying than that, while I was writing about the need for gender equality, a court in Spain cleared five men of raping a child because she was unconscious so they didn't need to use violence.

In the trial for the murder of Grace Millane, killed while backpacking in New Zealand, Grace's sexual history was used as evidence for the defence. And in December, the charity Beat released updated guidance to help people with an eating disorder over Christmas. There is indeed a long way to go.

Centuries of gender inequality can't be undone overnight, but every day there are stories of women and men who are doing their best to fight the entrenched social stigmas and rules that we all labour under. Girls at my school are more engaged in politics than I've ever seen them. My students tell me about standing up for their sex-based rights on an almost daily basis, whether it's correcting misconceptions online, calling out their parents when they behave in a biased way, or being brave enough to openly call themselves feminist when others seek to make that a dirty word.

I haven't put any suggestion in this book that isn't possible – every one is currently working somewhere in the country. Some people reading this will have the whole-school leadership role or responsibility to make it happen. And there's no doubt that some of the approaches need a school to stand up and say as one body, "We are a feminist place of work and education." Lots of these suggestions, though, are easy for individual teachers to start talking about and working towards.

We can all reflect on how we interact with students and check our unconscious bias. We can all start to see the way we educate male and female students as feminist. At its core, feminism is about creating equality by lifting everybody up and allowing them to be themselves, without trying to force them into a set of behaviours or feelings based on biology.

A feminist education benefits everyone. It empowers women to step forward and take their equal place in the workplace and at home. It empowers men to do the same. It values the feminine attributes that can make our society kinder, more nurturing, more caring, more compassionate. It says to everybody: you matter. In our daily practice in schools, we can take a more feminist approach to education that encourages students to be more ambitious for their future selves, in work and at home, and model the society that will enable them to flourish.

Acknowledgements

Thank you to everyone who has helped me shape me ideas for this book, which feels like it has been a long time coming. In particular, the following:

I'm grateful for the support and encouragement of so many people on EduTwitter, far too many to count, who've sent positive messages, been enthusiastic about the content, and given up time to read and provide feedback. You've helped to make this a better book: thank you so much.

Thanks to all the staff and students I've worked with at Skipton Girls' High School – virtually every interaction over the past decade has fed into the thinking here. It's a privilege to work with such dedicated people, especially my English colleagues, who are always ready to discuss literature, pedagogy and feminism, as well as the best swear words!

For the girls, Fiona, Mags and Lucy, who've got my back forever and always, and are always ready with a feminist gif to soothe the outrage, because laughter is often the best weapon.

Thanks to my family, for the unconditional love and support, the strong women and the feminist men. I love you all immensely.

And for Dan, for all your unwavering love and belief in me, and endless support for me and the things I do.